Bringing
Speech
to Life

A Companion Workbook to
Louis Colaianni's THE JOY OF PHONETICS AND ACCENTS

Claudia Anderson   Louis Colaianni

JOY PRESS
2002

Anderson, Claudia and Louis Colaianni
    Bringing speech to life: a companion workbook to Louis Colaianni's the joy of phonetics and accents / by Claudia Anderson and Louis Colaianni.

    ISBN 0-9727450-1-7 : $22.50
    1. English language—Pronunciation by foreign speakers.
    2. Acting. 3. English language—Phonetics. 4. Voice culture.

<h1>TABLE OF CONTENTS</h1>

ACKNOWLEDGEMENTS

We would like to thank: Kelly C. McAndrew, our chief editorial assistant, with a natural gift for articulation; Bonnie Raphael for her many helpful comments and for coming up with the perfect title for this book; Cal Pritner, Chair Theatre Department, University of Missouri-Kansas City for going above and beyond the call of duty in his support of this project; the Theater faculty of UMKC; the staff at the Missouri Repertory Theater; Ralph Pine and Ina Kohler for taking an interest in this venture; Dana Vranic for her many suggestions and hours of typing; Rick Wasserman for suggesting the "Variable O" list; Pamela Absten who went over the workbook page by page, asked probing quesitons and encouraged the writing at every stage; the speech students at CalArts, who used the workbook in its many incarnations, brought to it new ideas and gave practical suggestions; the faculty at CalArts, particularly voice faculty Fran Bennett, Irene Connors and Chris DeMore, who provided an arena for the imaginative teaching of speech and dialects; Ruth Rootberg, who read the earliest draft and called our attention to strengths and weaknesses; Tina Packer and the faculty of Shakespeare & Company's January and June workshops where the individual's connection to language is nurtured and celebrated; Judy Shahn, Trudie Kessler and Deb Hale for support for the ideas and the writing of the workbook. Finally, thank you to Kristin Linklater who has rethought the art of teaching and inspired a new generation of teachers.

Introduction

This workbook offers a creative, personal approach to working with the sounds of the English Language. It is designed to be used with *The Joy of Phonetics and Accents* (Drama Publishers, 1994.) The written exercises give you the opportunity to let the experiential work with Phonetic Pillows flow down through your arm and out onto the page, so that written symbols represent your experience of sound. The progression of activities begins with non-judgemental play with the shapes of the International Phonetic Alphabet (IPA) symbols. There is a page for each sound, giving you the opportunity to draw the sound while speaking it. As you speak sounds, make drawings of them and even color them, you can personalize each sound and deepen your relationship with it. As you explore your use of sounds in words, you will become aware of your own habitual pronunciations. If you are working with other people, you will be able to compare your own pronunciations to others' pronunciations.

The exercises in this workbook are not about "getting it right" or learning "standard" pronunciations, but, rather, are intended to increase your self-awareness and to expand your sound vocabulary and range of choices. As in The *Joy of Phonetics and Accents*, the IPA is used to explore sounds, to expand awareness of language and to compare differences in accents rather than to set a standard for speaking. Not only is the work fun, but it is useful in developing intelligibility, openness, vocal freedom and sensitivity to the relationships between sound, sense, and feeling. The Phonetic Pillows, three-dimensional, "huggable" and "throwable," help you to connect your interior experience of sound with a kinesthetic feeling of the Phonetic Alphabet. The sounds of language, experienced in your body as vibrations of sound, experienced by your eyes as written shapes, can be touched as well as seen. They can be shared by two or more people--used in communication.

If you are to use the Phonetic Alphabet to describe your own accent and to acquire new accents, the act of **writing** phonetic symbols while **speaking** the sounds is a logical step in the process. **Drawing** the shapes of the symbols while holding and touching the sounds and feeling their vibrations travelling through your body will help you to remember these symbols and to form relationships with them. This workbook will help you to expand your relationships with sounds and to use the sounds more effectively in language.

The Creative Process

A performing artist needs to uncover or rediscover his/her connections to sound and word if he/she is to use language to embody experience. The creative process requires experiential approaches, time to explore and opportunities to use childlike imagination. In many cases, the artist is counteracting years of educational conditioning in which the learning process was based solely on linear thinking, logical patterns and prescriptive views. Many books have been published, and workshops developed, on the theory of the creative process. *The Artist's Way*, by Julia Cameron, *Writing the Natural Way*, by Gabriele Lusser Rico and *Drawing on the Artist Within*, by Betty Edwards are just a few of the many books which have as their objectives to nurture the creative process, particularly when it has been blocked. At the beginning of the process, the artist needs to "quell the painful critic," says Rico, and "reawaken and cultivate some of the ways we had of perceiving and expressing when we were children...to 'return to beginner's mind, to the child state, to Beingness prior to conditioned and memorized ideas about life.'" Methods such as "clustering" in writing or drawing with the non-dominant hand for painters suggest that the path to artistry is not necessarily a direct, straight, logical one. In order for artists to grow, they need to experience, expand awarenesses, unblock primitive impulse, awaken childlike imagination, free their instincts to create. An actor (or any performing artist who uses language) needs access to a wide variety of experiences with language. Before a cultivated, specific use of language is asked for, some freedom is necessary. Language is useless unless it describes experience--unless it includes emotional and physical involvement.

Inspired by Linklater

The physical approach to speech and phonetics outlined in *The Joy of Phonetics and Accents* and further explored in this workbook is intended to complement and augment the freeing process of the Linklater voice progression. Kristin Linklater writes, in *Freeing Shakespeare's Voice*:

"The vowels and consonants of the English language have been badly treated over the last hundred years. I don't mean that 'good speech has deteriorated,' I mean that artificial standards of 'correct speech' have associated any mention of vowels and consonants with judgments of correct and incorrect, good or bad, upper or lower class, intelligent or stupid, educated or illiterate. Most speech training employs the International Phonetic[s] Alphabet to analyze regionalisms and train the ear to change individual usage. Phonetics is the science of sounds, the orthographic representation of vocal sounds. It was invented some hundred fifty years ago to attempt a more accurate spelling system for the English language. It failed to catch on as spelling but remained to be refined as a system for distinguishing the different sound usage in different languages and dialects. The I.P.A. is a sophisticated scientific language tool which has been overused in speech-training for actors to the detriment of the aesthetics of language. The beauty of a vowel does not lie in the correctness of its pronunciation according to some arbitrary standard; it lies in its intrinsic musicality, its sensuality, its expressiveness. Vowels are compounded from the vibrations of the human voice molded by subtle changes in the shape of the channels through which those vibrations flow. As the channels narrow or broaden, get larger or smaller, the vibrations change both shape and pitch to create the fundamental elements of the music of speech. When the vowel pitches mix with inflections of thought the result is kaleidoscopic harmony. Consciously or unconsciously, a great poet uses the sounds within words to communicate mood and accentuate meaning. Shakespeare's use of words can paint scenery, change day into night, provoke attack and evoke emotions, not only through imagery but through the sounds that make the words that hold the imagery. Consonants and vowels are sensory agents of speech communicating information on sound waves which carry subliminal messages from speaker to listener. Twentieth-century listeners are conditioned to translate what they hear more cerebrally than in the age of oral communication, but 'whole-body' speaking is still operative even though we may not be consciously tuned in to it."

In her quest to promote "full-body speaking" in actor training, Linklater developed <u>Sound & Movement</u>, a lively alternative to traditional speech work. The Phonetic Pillow process was directly inspired by this work. The Sound & Movement process demands full-body involvement, in contrast with "good speech" pedagogy which emphasizes only what goes on from the neck up. Linklater writes of Sound & Movement: "If we are to tackle eloquence as opposed to elocution, we must approach language with courage ... take words back to physical and emotional sources ... give our bodies to images and let ***the feel of the words*** be the motor of our movements ... in having the voice and body simultaneously available as two channels of expression, there is the opportunity for a much richer release of imaginative energy."

Unlike traditional speech work, the Sound & Movement process is in no way sedentary; it includes the entire body. In one Sound & Movement exercise, the body is envisioned as a hollow vessel through which voice vibrations flow and fuel the body into movement. The progression of Sound & Movement exercises includes the strong imagery of color. Actors are asked to imagine the color red, for instance, entering their body "through their breath and flowing immediately to the emotional receiving and transmitting center of the solar plexus, where the breath transforms to voice vibrations which then flow back out through any and all of the channels of the body," thereby energizing, enlivening and moving the body. The progression finally leads to the sounds of language. One after another, actors explore and discover the inherent qualities of *u, æ, i, b, s, m, g*, etc. until all of the components of language, one at a time, have been activated through the body. These building blocks of language are then joined (articulated) into words, phrases and speeches. Through visceral availability and immediacy, the words are rediscovered, almost reinvented by the actor. The result is fresh, exuberant communication which is emotionally charged and intellectually acute.

Inspired by Early Learning

A similar process has been highly effective in elementary education for many years. Rudolf Steiner developed a system of eurythmy which recognized inherent attributes in each sound of language and expressed them through movement. In the eurythmy class children learn to "dance" sounds and words long before learning to read and write. Maria Montessori developed the "movable alphabet" which consists of large sandpaper cut-outs of the letters of the alphabet. Pre-literate children trace the shapes of each letter in order to prepare the hand muscles for writing. The children also learn to arrange letters into words along a lined surface. The Phonetic Pillow approach actually merges aspects of Steiner's inner spiritual relationship to sound with Montessori's outwardly practical methods of preparing the student to read and write. For the actor, the Phonetic Pillow approach bridges experiential, process-oriented voice work and the symbol-based, phonetic exactitude of speech training.

With our students, we have invented many games using Phonetic Pillows, and Voice and Speech teachers around the US are constantly adding more games to the list. It is the experience of teachers we have interviewed that students remember the symbols more readily, get higher quiz grades and achieve a sensual experience of language. Teachers have observed that students who formerly viewed phonetics as tedious, dull and confining actually look forward to phonetics classes.

By gearing the study of phonetics toward the physicality of other performance classes, student actors not only retain symbols better, but use them more creatively in the study of stage accents. In combination with voice-freeing exercises, phonetics helps to open and develop the actor's voice. It isn't necessary to emphasize "standard speech" because Sound & Movement-based explorations with Phonetic Pillows help students to achieve maximum intelligibility, openness and vocal versatility. They lose the limitations of regionalisms without having the life's blood of individuality drained from their voices.

The International Phonetic Alphabet (IPA)

It is the conviction of the authors that there is not an absolute, pure pronunciation for each phoneme in the International Phonetic Alphabet which the individual must perfect through practice. The American Heritage Dictionary defines "phoneme," as the smallest phonetic unit in a language that is capable of communicating a distinction in meaning, such as *m* in *mat* vs. *b* in *bat*." The sound of a phoneme is altered slightly by the context of the word in which it occurs. This happens because the organs of speech are in action; they have moved from the formation of the previous phoneme and must adapt to the formation of the next phoneme. For example, the / u / in "pool" is not exactly the same as the / u / in "shoot."

If you were to examine the work of individual phoneticians, linguists and speech teachers who have used the IPA to describe language and/or to prescribe pronunciations, you would find that each person seems to operate within his or her own set of rules. Each system describes which symbols are used to represent which sounds, how exactly they are drawn, how nuance markings are used and how punctuation is indicated. There exists an International Phonetics Alphabet Association as well as documents describing various rules, but not everyone follows these. There are several pronouncing dictionaries using the IPA, which were either written expressly for actors or have been found useful by actors; among them are Kenyon and Knott's *A Pronouncing Dictionary of American English*, Daniel Jones' *English Pronunciation,* and J.C. Wells' *Longman's Pronounciiation Dictionary.* Each dictionary contains its own internal consistencies. The examples and passages written in IPA in this workbook will come from these dictionaries. You may, therefore, check your accuracy against multiple choices of pronunciation found in these books.

INTRODUCTION TO PHONETIC SYMBOLS

Here are some of the symbols of the International Phonetic Alphabet as they appear in *The Joy of Phonetics and Accents*.

i ɪ ɛ æ a ɑ ə ʌ ɚ ɝ ɒ ɔ o ʊ u aɪ ɔɪ aʊ

oʊ eɪ o e ju b p g k d t v f h ʤ j l m n r s

ʃ w ð θ z ʒ ŋ ʧ hw

Here are some additional symbols of the International Phonetic Alphabet:

ɾ ʈ ʀ ʔ ʓ β ɨ ʘ œ ɸ t y x χ !

They are used in various accents and languages.

Write each symbol below so that it is readable, neat and consistent. Written symbols should contain all of the elements necessary to communicate each specific IPA symbol: shape, height and position on the line (some symbols, / j /, / g /, / p /, / ʃ /, / ʒ /, / ŋ /, / ʤ /, / ʧ / dip below the line.) Consider yourself an artist who is copying the work of a master artist for communication with other artists. As you write each symbol, speak the sound aloud, and imagine an experience of the sound flowing through your body down your arm onto the page. If you have already worked with Phonetic Pillows, imagine the feel and shape as you touched them. Do you have the sound of the symbol in your ear already? You may have discovered that one or two of the sounds in the key word list below does not correspond with your "accent." In those cases, you may choose to expand your accent to use those sounds, or reserve them for use in stage accents.

typed symbol	my script	key words
i	_____	sea, eat
ɪ	_____	fit, sick
eɪ	_____	play, age
ɛ	_____	edge, bet
æ	_____	cat, ran, ask*, dance*
ɑ	_____	father, spa, odd**
ə	_____	alert, account
ʌ	_____	abrupt, up
ɚ	_____	dinner, water
ɝ	_____	squirm, search
ɒ	_____	odd**, possible**
ɔ	_____	bought**, wall**
o	_____	omit, obey
ʊ	_____	wool, pudding
u	_____	group, doodle

*pronounced with / a / or / ɑ / in some accents. See Appendix 1 "The Variable A."

**pronounced with / ɑ / or / ɒ / in some accents. See Appendix 2 "The Variable O."

aɪ	——	style, might
ɔɪ	——	choice, joy
aʊ	——	house, brown
oʊ	——	toast, old
ju	——	you, duke
b	——	brown, feeble
p	——	peel, ape
g	——	vulgar, green
k	——	risk, quietly
d	——	pleased, data
t	——	taste, must
v	——	victory, love
f	——	offer, photo
h	——	hello, ahoy
ʤ	——	message, gypsy
ʧ	——	check, arch
l	——	lack, quickly
m	——	damsel, mood
n	——	down, knee
r	——	roar, priest
s	——	taste, street
ʃ	——	usher, shy
j	——	yellow, youth
w	——	away, west
ð	——	smooth, those

9

θ	_____	**both, think**
z	_____	jazz, prisms
ʒ	_____	casual, vision
ŋ	_____	si**ng**, **ang**uish
hw	_____	**wh**ite, over**wh**elm

The more you "practice" writing in IPA, the clearer the connection between sound and symbol will be for you. Your written IPA will embody your experience. As you begin to remember how to write the symbols, they will begin to have meaning for you. As you practice, your response to the symbol will become more immediate, so that the IPA will be more useful as a tool for communicating--with yourself, other actors, directors and voice and speech directors.

VOWELS

EXPRESSIVE DRAWING

For the next exercise, You will be asked to make an expressive drawing of each phonetic symbol. You will need crayons, colored markers or colored pencils to draw each phonetic symbol. Obtain some good, thick art paper, or a tablet for drawing so that you can devote an 8-by-12 inch page to each symbol.

You will be asked to draw and color each symbol while speaking it; feeling it move through your body, your senses and your memory. Let the shape of your drawing be recognizable as the shape of the IPA symbol; color and design it to reflect your feeling as the sound travles through your body. When you are finished oloring all of the symbols, you can use these renderings as flash cards or pillow-substitues for practice in recallingthe sound of each symbol. Use the back-side of each drawing to write key words which contain that sound, or notes to help you remember that symbol. Take time to deepen your relationship with each of the sounds. The questions which accompany each sound in this exercise are intended to stimulate your memories, your imagination and your playful exploration. Invent an answer to each question, even if an answer does not immediately come to you.

u

Use a whole page to draw / u / . Color it with colored pencils, crayons or markers. Speak the sound aloud as you color it. Ruminate on / u / as you use your creativity in the drawing and coloring of it. Allow your imagination fluidity as you draw and color. Then, answer the questions below.

----How does this sound make you feel?

-----What part of your body do the vibrations of / u / seem to want as you draw and speak it?

----Write as many words as you can think of that contain the sound / u /.

ʊ

Use another whole page to draw and color / ʊ /. Trace its shape as you give it your full voice. Look for vibrations in your body.

----How does this sound make you feel?

-----Write several / ʊ / words here.

----What might the shape of the sound remind you of?

-----What part of your body do the vibrations of / ʊ / seem to occupy as you draw and speak it?

Draw and color / ɔ / . Allow your imagination to take off as you draw and color. Speak the sound on low, rumbling vibrations of your voice. Call the sound out of the middle of your body as you speak it again. Speak it again on higher pitches of your voice.

----What feelings are released when you speak this sound?

----Look in the mirror as you say this sound. Are your lips rounded?

-----/ ɔ / is a relatively long sound. How does it feel different if you make it short?

ɒ

Draw and color / ɒ / . Refer to page 143 in *The Joy of Phonetics and Accents* for some words that may contain this sound. For a complete understanding of words with this sound, refer to Appendix 2 "The Variable O." Ponder the / ɒ / as you draw and color it.

-----Do you use this sound in "on," "not," "honest," odd," or "god?" If / ɒ / is not your usual pronunciation in these words, which sound do you use for the vowel in those words?

-----/ ɒ / is an intrinsically short sound. It's sometimes called the "short o" because many words that use this vowel are spelled with an "o." Write five other words in which you could use this sound.

OƱ

Draw and color / oʊ / with colored pencils, crayons or markers. Turn / oʊ / over and over in your mind as you draw and color it. Speak it, allowing the vibrations of sound to move your body. Let the sound flow down your arm and onto your page. Feel the change in resonance in your mouth as the / o / makes its transition into / ʊ / in the formation of this diphthong. For more information on diphthongs, see pages 10-12 in *The Joy of Phonetics and Accents*.

----How does this sound make you feel? Could it express an emotion all by itself?

-----In what words might you use this diphthong / oʊ /? Write five of them here.

----What personality does / oʊ / have? Describe it as if it were a character.

ɑ

Whisper / ɑ /. Then let the sound have the vibrations of your voice as you draw / ɑ /. Allow your imagination to wander as you draw and color.

----If this sound had a temperature, would it be hot or cold?

___You might speak this sound as "aaaaaahhh." What might that express for you?

-----Write six words that you pronounce with the vowel / ɑ / here.

----Does the shape of the symbol encourage you to draw the sound out of your body on vibrations of your voice?

Sound Break: More practice with / ɑ /, / ɒ /, / ɔ /, / oʊ /, / ʊ /, and / u /.

See if you can recall the sounds you have drawn on the preceding pages as they are found in words. Write the IPA symbol for the **vowel sound** in each of the following words.

father   _____

school   _____

saw   _____

through   _____

sought   _____

slosh   _____

probe   _____

foot   _____

doom   _____

calm   _____

stone   _____

Write one word containing each of the following sounds.

/ oʊ /   _____

/ ʊ /   _____

/ ɑ /   _____

/ ɒ /   _____

/ u /   _____

/ ɔ /   _____

"Unstable" Sounds

In any national or regional accent there are characteristic sounds which are commonly heard. For example, the vowel sounds used by most US speakers from different regions are similar enough that they are all recognized as American speech patterns. However, for a variety of sociological reasons, speakers from the same area may have different pronounciations in certain instances. These reasons may include ethnic and cultural influences and desire for prestige. The so called 'Harvard A' in a phrase like "ask the class to dance" is an unstable sound in American English. It is used to a limited extent in one region of the country. But has been adopted in Academia and in the Theater as a mark of high status. Most Americans, however, never use this sound. For more information, see Appendix 1 "The Variable A."

Another, perhaps less dramatic, example of an unstable sound is the presence or lack of lip rounding in the vowel of words like LAW. The boundaries on this type of sound can be regionally drawn, but even within the same region some speakers will be heard to say / lɔ / and others will be heard to say / lɑ /. In fact the rounded AW sound / ɔ / does not exist in all accents of American English and can therefore be called "unstable." It is useful to become familiar with which sounds tend to be "unstable" or changeable. Knowledge of unstable and esoteric sounds will give you confidence in your own accent. It will also make you aware of alternate choices for pronunciation. This will enable you to make more informed choices in your speaking as an actor.

Dictionaries and pronouncing lexicons can be used as guides for both contemporary and antiquated pronunciation patterns. Each dictionary has its own objectives, sometimes descriptive, sometimes prescriptive; in other words, sometimes a dictionary shows you how the authors think the word ought to be pronounced and sometimes they show you the results of their research into common usage. If you want to know how a word was pronounced in a certain period, you may want to use a dictionary published during that period. The authors will usually indicate whether or not they attempt to preserve a particular pronunciation, or to reflect the pronunciation most people are currently using.

/ ɑ / or / ɒ / or / ɔ /

Distinguishing among these three sounds can be difficult for some English speakers. Do you use the same vowel or a different voewl in each of these words: calm, wash, law. American speakers vary widely in the pronunciation of such words. At first, they may sound rather alike to you. Speech students sometimes say, "I'm confused about all the "A" sounds."

It will be useful for you to have all three sounds in your sound vocabulary, even if you don't usually use them in your everyday speech. In isolation, / ɑ / is the most open, relaxed sound; there is no lip-rounding or tongue-tension. / ɔ / has distinct lip-rounding and the tongue is not completely relaxed. If you were to speak "aaaahhhhh" and then "awwwww," you might be able to feel the difference in your lips and in your body. Allow the difference to be more than merely a difference in tension in your lips and tongue. See if your emotional response is different. See if the pitches are different.

/ ɒ / is an unstable vowel in many accents of English. Speakers of many accents don't use it at all; others use it inconsistently, while still others use it all the time. This is the short, lip-rounded vowel which can be heard in New England, and some Western and Northern states in words like ODD, LOT, STOP and WHAT. In many US accents, these words are pronounced with the vowel / ɑ / or sometimes / a /.You might think of the sound of / ɒ / as halfway between / ɑ / and / ɔ / in terms of lip-rounding and tongue-tension. It is a short sound, whereas / ɑ / and / ɔ / are intrinsically long. This is a simplistic description of the differences, but it might help you in your initial distinction among the three sounds. In order to clarify the differences in the "unstable" sounds, refer to pages 34-40 from Part One in *The Joy of Phonetics and Accents*. Also read "The Use of / ɒ / or / ɑ / in Short O Words" on page 58 in Part Four of *The Joy of Phonetics*. (For more information, see Appendix 2 "The Variable O.")

Notice how you speak the words. Is the sound long? Do you use / ɑ /? Do you use the / ɑ /, but shorten it? Are your lips relaxed as for / ɑ / or slightly rounded as in / ɒ /?

Which vowel sound do you use in the capitalized words in this sentence from "The Undiapered Filefish," from Part Five in *The Joy of Phonetics and Accents* ?

WHAT COMEDY, this NOD to the POSSIBLE INVOLVEMENT of GOD is the religion of the ODD COLLEGE SCHOLAR.

/ ɑ / or / ɒ /?

_____COMEDY

_____NOD

_____POSSIBLE

_____INVOLVEMENT

_____GOD

_____ODD

_____COLLEGE

_____SCHOLAR

_____WHAT (or do you use / ʌ / ?)

How about these words, from several of Shakespeare's Sonnets?:

_____STOP

_____COMPOSITION

_____ON

_____CHOPPED

_____DOCTORLIKE

_____ROBBING

_____MOCK

/ ɔ / is unstable in many accents of English. In words like COUGH, ALL and SAW the speakers of many accents don't use it at all, some use it inconsistently, others use it all the time. If you come from the Northwestern U.S., you are likely to say / kɑf /, / ɑl / and / sɑ /. If you come from New York City, you are likely to say / kɔf /, / ɔl / and / sɔ /.

Which vowel sound do you use in the capitalized words in the following sentence from *The Unciapered Filefish* from part five of *The Joy of Phonetics and Accents*?

"They BOUGHT the bit of WALL at the AUCTION."

_____BOUGHT

_____WALL

_____AUCTION

Notice how you say the following capitalized words. Do you round your lips and use a long sound as in / ɔ /? Are your lips relaxed as in / ɑ /? Do you round your lips a bit and shorten the vowel as in / ɒ /?

Sonnet 71
"And MOCK you with me after I am GONE."

_____MOCK

_____GONE

Sonnet 73
"This thou perceiv'st, which makes thy love more STRONG,
To love that well which thou must leave ere LONG."

_____STRONG

_____LONG

Sonnet 77
"These OFFICES, so OFT as thou wilt look,
Shall PROFIT thee, and much enrich thy book."

_____OFFICES

_____OFT

_____PROFIT

Sonnet 92
"But what's so blessed-fair that fears no BLOT?
Thou mayst be FALSE, and yet I know it NOT."

_____BLOT

_____FALSE

_____NOT

Sonnet 114
"And that your love taught it this alchemy,
To make of MONSTERS, and things indigest,
Such cherubins as your sweet self resemble,
Creating every bad a perfect best
As fast as OBJECTS to his beams assemble?"

_____MONSTERS

_____OBJECTS

Try substituting an alternate vowel sound for MONSTERS and OBJECTS--one that is not your habit. Does it make a difference to you in context of the lines?

Using colored pencils, crayons or markers, make a wash of color that feels like / ɔ / to you right now.

Choose a different color for / ɒ /.

Without thinking, choose a different color for / ɑ /.

Λ

Use a whole page to draw / Λ / . Speak it several times as you draw with your colored pencils, crayons or markers. Mull over the sound of / Λ / as you draw and color it.

-----Read scene / Λ / from "The Undiapered Filefish" on page 149 of *The Joy of Phonetics and Accents*. Then speak all of the capitalized words. In that scene, what English-spelling letters are used in those capitalized words for the sound / Λ /?

The shape of a symbol sometimes literally symbolizes the mouth formation of the sound it represents. For example / i / is said to indicate a high tongue position becasue the dot represents a point on the roof of the mouth and the straight line, an upward arrow indicates a high tongue position.
-----Invent a connection between the shape of the phonetic symbol / Λ / and its sound.

-----What adjectives come to your mind as you draw / Λ /? Write four or five adjectives containing / Λ / that describe you.

Draw / ə /. Adopt an adept vision of / ə / as you use your creativity in the drawing and coloring of it. Allow your imagination to adjust to this sound.

The following words contain one or more / ə /. Underline the syllables where they occur. The first two are transcribed into IPA so that you can see where the / ə / occurs.

SECRET   / sikrət /

AGAIN   / əgɛn /

LIKABLE

IMPLACABLE

FRACAS

ELIMINATED

ADJOINING

MINUTES

ALLOW

PLIABLE

Multisyllabic words often have the / ə / vowel in very weak syllables. Read the following words, written in IPA:

   ɪntə'lɛktʃuəl   plætə'tudɪnəs   fɔr'tuɪtəsnəs   plə'tounɪəm   æntaɪdɪsə'stæblɪʃmən'tɛrɪənɪzm

Read the following sentence, written in IPA, noting the occurrences of / ə /. How many are there?

/ ðə laɪt blaɪndəd ðəm, bət ðeɪ wɝ dɪtɝmnd tə wɑtʃ ðə sʌnraɪz /

ɝ

Draw and color / ɝ / . Allow your imagination to take a journey as you draw and color.

-----How does this sound feel going through you?

-----Do you feel your tongue responding as it gets the message for / ɝ / ? What action does your tongue seem to take?

-----Here are words containing / ɝ /. Underline the syllables where the / ɝ / occurs. Two of the words are transcribed into IPA so that you can see where the / ɝ / occurs.

PERFECT (the adjective)

PURR

SQUIRM

SKIRMISH

FERMENT (the noun)

MURDER   / mɝdɚ /

IMMERSION

PREFER   / prɪfɝ /

WERE

SIR

OCCUR

-----Write five more words that contain / ɝ /.

Draw and color / ɚ /. Feel the sound / ɚ / as you draw and color it.

Spell these words containing / ɚ / in English here.

/ rɪvɚ /_____

/ snɪkɚd /_____

/ lusɚ /_____

/ slækɚ /_____

/ mɪrɚ /_____

-----Write the / ɚ / words from "Scene / ɚ / on page 131 from "The Undiapered Filefish" in *The Joy of Phonetics and Accents*. Underline the syllables that contain the / ɚ /.

Sounds in Action: More practice with / ʌ /, / ə /, / ɝ / and / ɚ /.

Perhaps you've noticed that / ʌ / and / ə / sound alike (or similar) and that / ɝ / and / ɚ / sound alike (or similar) when sounded by themselves rather than as parts of words.

/ ʌ / and / ə /

Read Scene / ə / on page 150 of *The Joy of Phoenetics and Accents*. Compare the capitalized words with those in Scene / ʌ / on page 149 of *The Joy of Phoenetics and Accents*. What is the difference in the two sounds as they occur in words?

So that you can practice distinguishing between the two sounds, / ʌ / and / ə /, write several words containing / ʌ / here:

_____ _____ _____ _____ _____ _____

and write several words containing / ə / here:

_____ _____ _____ _____ _____ _____

In order to distinguish the two sounds, you must sense the rhythm of a word--the relationship of stressed syllables to unstressed syllables. Stressed syllables usually receive greater loudness than unstressed syllables; they may also be distinguished by elongation or higher pitch. Read the two scenes again. Which element do you use for stressed syllables--loudness, pitch, elongation or a combination of two or three elements?

Here are several words containing both sounds. Speak them aloud, feel them move through your body and your mouth.

ABRUPT   SUCCUMB   ABUT   ADJUST   AVUNCULAR

When you speak the words, is one vowel sound louder than the other? Is it / ʌ / or / ə /?

Is one of these two vowel sounds longer than the other?

Is one of these two vowel sounds higher in pitch than the other?

/ ɝ / and / ɚ /

Read Scene / ɝ / on page 132 in Part Five in *The Joy of Phonetics and Accents*. All of the capitalized words in this scene contain / ɝ /.

Read Scene / ɚ / on page 150 of *The Joy of Phoenetics and Accents*. Compare the capitalized words with those in Scene / ɝ /. Note the difference in stress of the two sounds as they occur in words. Which of the sounds is appropriate for stressed syllables?

So that you can practice distinguishing between the two sounds, / ɝ / and / ɚ /, write several words containing / ɝ / here:

_____ _____ _____ _____ _____ _____

and write several words containing / ɚ / here:

_____ _____ _____ _____ _____ _____

Here are several words containing both sounds. Speak them aloud, feel them move through your body and your mouth.

MURDER   FURTHER   GIRDER   PERTURB   PERJURE

Are you clear about when to use the stressed versions of the sounds / ɝ / and / ʌ / and when to use the unstressed sounds / ɚ / and / ə / ?

If the word is monosyllabic (one syllable) would you use the stressed sound or the unstressed?

How do you know when to use an unstressed representation of the sound?

/ɜ/ and /ə/ as variants of /ɝ/ and /ɚ/

Accents of the English Language vary when it comes to the use of / ɝ / and / ɚ /. Some English speakers speak the two sounds with "strong R Coloring," and some with little or no "R Coloring." For the vowels you have just explored, "R Coloring" is represented by a little tail or flag attached to the vowel. For more information on "R Coloring", see pages 81-89. There is more about R in the consonant section of this work book. You can also refer to Part Four in *The Joy of Phonetics and Accents* for a discussion of "R Coloring." The vowel / ɚ / without "R Coloring" is transcribed as / ə /. The vowel / ɝ / without "R Coloring" is transcribed as / ɜ /.

Are you aware of your use of "R Coloring" in comparison with people you know? In some parts of the American Southeast, some parts of the American Northeast, some parts of Great Britain, etc. the sounds used are / ɜ /, in words like Bird and / ə /, in words like Moth<u>er</u>. Do you use these sounds in your everyday speech?

Whom in your class or among your friends uses these sounds?

Part Four in *The Joy of Phonetics and Accents* deals with pronunciation contrasts among different accents of English. There are many varieties in the use of the consonant / r / as well as in the use of the vowels / ɝ /, / ɜ /, / ɚ /and / ə / . Some people tap the r sound, some trill, some people form the r sound further back in the mouth and some further forward. Listen to different languages and you'll hear great differences in the formation of r. Listen to your classmates or friends and you'll hear more subtle differences. People often refer to speech as having a "soft" or a "hard" R sound, which can affect the consonant sound of / r / as well as the vowel sounds around it. The opposite of the lack of "R Coloring" is a strong R or "hard R" sound. People from parts of Ireland, Texas, the American Southeast and the American Midwest often use a more vigorous r sound.

Whom among your friends uses a "hard" R sound?

i

Draw and color / i / . Speak the sound and feel / i / stream through your arms and legs as you draw and color it.

-----Describe an early memory of this sound--from your childhood.

-----What words come to your mind as you draw / i /? Write a sentence here that contains four or five words with / i /.

_____

_____

-----Is there anything about the shape of this symbol that could remind you of its sound? Invent a way to remember the sound of this symbol.

I

Draw and color / ɪ / . Let / ɪ / whip through your body and tickle your tongue as you draw and color it. Allow your imagination to take wing.

-----What is the first word that comes to your mind as you draw / ɪ /?

-----How will you remember the difference between / ɪ / and / i / ? Create an image or a mneumonic device for yourself.

-----Write a short poem using / ɪ / and / i / words.

Draw / ɛ / . Celebrate the sound of / ɛ / as you draw and color it. Revel in the sound.

-----What words come to your mind as you draw / ɛ /? "Do you use the sound in "fester," "gentle," "crest," "steady," "blessed," or "when?" Write a sentence here that contains four or five words with / ɛ /.

_____

_____

-----The vowel / ɛ / is intrinsically a short sound. Let each of several parts of your body speak this sound: your hand, your forehead, your knee, your shoulder, etc. Which part of your body seems to suit the personality of / ɛ /?

eɪ

Draw the diphthong / eɪ /. Weigh the sound of / eɪ / as you draw and color it. Play around in the sound.

-----What images come to mind as you say the sound?

----What action words come to your mind as you draw / eɪ /? Write five of them here.

-----Write the following words in English spelling here.

/ pleɪ / _____

/ teɪm /_____

/ seɪ / _____

/ pleɪs /_____

/ feɪk / _____

/ weɪ / _____

/ feɪməs /_____

/ reɪz / _____

Draw and color / æ / . Splash it across the page.

-----What is the first word that comes to you when you play the sound through your body? Write some rhyming words as well.

-----If you were to personify the sound, or give / æ / a characterization, what would it be? Describe an imagined character.

-----Write a short monologue for this character using ten words containing / æ /.

a

Draw / a / . Engraft the sound of / a / onto your senses as you draw and color it. Let your vast imagination dance as you let the sound play through you onto the page.

----- Do you use the sound / a / in the words "ask," "aunt," "rather," "laugh," "waft," or "enchanted?" Perhaps you sometimes or always use / æ / for these words; perhaps you use / a / only in certain situations. For more information about / a / refer to pages 34-40 in *The Joy of Phonetics*. Also, see Appendix 1 "The Variable A."

-----Write a sentence here that contains four or five words which could be pronounced using / a /.

_____

_____

Personalize: More practice with / a /, / æ /, / eɪ /, / ɛ /, / ɪ /, and / i /.
/ a / and / æ /

Review pages 34 to 40 in Part One of *The Joy of Phonetics and Accents* (also read pages 58-59 and look at the contrasts among accents on pages 112-117.) The use of these two sounds depends on your accent. You may use / æ / in words where others would use / a /.

/ a / is an unstable sound in many accents of English. "Unstable" means that it is not used at all in the accents of many speakers, others use it inconsistently, while still others use it all the time. (See page 58 of *The Joy of Phonetics and Accents* for more information about unstable sounds). Many speakers from New England use the sound / a / in such words as CAN'T, ASK, CLASS, DANCE, etc. (See Appendix 1 "The Variable A")

/ æ /, / a / or / ɑ /
What is your habit in your accent? Write the symbol you use in the blanks below.

Sonnet 131   "In nothing art thou black save in thy deeds
                         And thence this slander, as I think, proceeds."

_____SLANDER

Sonnet 123   "Our dates are brief, and therefore we admire
                         What thou dost foist upon us that is old,
                         And rather make them born to our desire
                         Than think that we before have heard them told.

_____RATHER

Sonnet 99   "The roses fearfully on thorns did stand,
                         One blushing shame, another white despair:"

_____STAND

How about the following words? Which sound do you use?

_____ASK

_____DANCE

_____DEMAND

_____PAST

_____LAUGH

/ ɛ / and / ɪ /

There are some variations in the use of the / ɛ / and / ɪ / among American speakers. Which do you use in the following words?

DENT   _____

TEN   _____

GEM   _____

LEND   _____

MEANT_____

Americans from the Southeast U.S. tend to use / ɪ / in these words; whereas most Americans use / ɛ /. How might this awareness be useful to you?

/ i / and / ɪ /

Most people who speak English as their first language are consistent in their choice of these two sounds within words, particularly in accented syllables. On the other hand, some Latino-Americans, whose first language is Spanish, may use them differently. Which sound do you use in the following words?

SIT   _____

SEAT   _____

FIT   _____

FEAT   _____

/ i / and / ɪ / sounds used in final "y" spellings.

Most speech texts and dictionaries employing the IPA use / ɪ / to indicate the final sound in the following words:

PRETTY, SORRY, PLENTY, RUSTY, SICKLY, INDUBITABLY

/ ɪ / is useful in indicating the unstressed value of the "y" at the ends of these words and it is accurate for old-fashioned varieties of English; however, it doesn't really reflect the modern pronunciation. / i / more accurately represents the pronunciation of most Americans.

Complete the following words using the vowel choice appropriate to your own accent:

/ prɪt   /,   / sɑr   /,   / plɛnt   /,   / rʌst   /,   /sɪkl   /,   /ɪndupɪtəbl   /

You may also find some variations in your pronunciations and those of your classmates for the first syllable of the following words:

BEFORE, BENEATH, REQUEST, SEQUESTER, PRESCRIBE, REMOVE

Do you pronounce the first syllable with / i / or with / ɪ / ? Or perhaps you use / ɘ / ?

ADDITIONAL
DIPHTHONGS
ɔɪ

Draw / ɔɪ /. Color it with colored pencils, crayons or markers. Enjoy the sound / ɔɪ / as you draw and color it. Let your imagination boil as you let the sound flow through you onto the page.

-----Let the diphthong make a journey in your body as it moves from / ɔ / to / ɪ /. Imagine that / ɔ / finds a channel in your body. Where in your body does the sound seem to go?

As you speak the dipthong / ɔɪ /, let the second element / ɪ /, find a different place in your body and let the sound move through that part of your body. Let the diphthong flow from the / ɔ / part of your body to the / ɪ / part of your body. Describe your experience.

Write five verbs that come to mind as you draw / ɔɪ /.

aI

---Let this sound take a journey in your body as it moves from / a / to / ɪ /. Let each of the two sounds of the diphthong find its own place in your body, as you did with / ɔɪ /. In which parts of your body does / aɪ / seem alive?

-----Turn your attention to the experience of your mouth with this sound. Do you feel your mouth changing shape to accommodate the different resonating shapes for the two sounds of this diphthong? What can you perceive about the acoustics of the two sounds?

-----What words come to your mind as you draw / aɪ /? Write two nouns, two verbs, two adjectives and two adverbs.

aʊ

Draw an / aʊ / . Color it with colored pencils, crayons or markers. Speak the sound / aʊ / aloud as you draw and color it. Let the sound empower you. Drown in the sound.

-----What happens in your mouth as the diphthong moves from / a / to / ʊ /? Do you feel your tongue and lips glide from the first sound into the second?

-----Do you sense a shift in where the sound seems to reside in your body as the diphthong moves from / a / to / ʊ /? Describe the sensation.

-----What words come to your mind as you draw / aʊ /? Write ten of them here.

O and e

In order to understand the symbols / o / and / e /, it is important to know the difference between a "pure vowel" and a "diphthong."

These are pure vowels: i, ɪ, e, ɛ, æ, a, ɑ, ʌ, ə, ɜ, ɒ, ɔ, o, ʊ, u

These are diphthongs: aɪ, ɔɪ, aʊ, eɪ, oʊ, ju

A diphthong is a combination of two pure vowels, which together, form a new sound. Before ending your exploration of the vowels, consider these shorter versions of the diphthongs you have learned as / oʊ / and / eɪ /. In their pronouncing dictionary, Kenyon and Knott use the symbols / o / and / e / versions to represent the diphthongs / oʊ / and / eɪ /. However, in *The Joy of Phoenetics*, this workbook and elsewhere, / o / and / e / are used to represent weaker, unstressed forms.

In the English language, particularly in American accents, the diphthongs / eɪ / and / oʊ / occur most often in stressed syllables and one-syllable words:

/ toʊst /	/ boʊt /	/ loʊ /	/ əfloʊt /	/ goʊ /
/ teɪm /	/ feɪməs /	/ ʃeɪmfʊl /	/ leɪm /	/ heɪnəs /

There are several words in English where the o sound occurs in unstressed positions and may be transcribed as follows:

/ oθɛloʊ /	/ obeɪ /	/ oblɪtəreɪt /	/ omɪt /	/ pozɛs /

Write three more words in which you might use the unaccented / o /.

The pure vowel / o / can be lengthened through diphthongization to / oʊ /. It can also be lengthened while retaining its pure vowel quality. The elongated pure vowel sound is useful for certain accents. For example, an Irish or Jamaican person may say:

/ toː st /	/ boː t /	/ loː /	/ əfloː t /	/ goː /

Notice the colon, the nauance marking for extra elongation.

The pure vowel / e / occurs in the French, Italian and Spanish languages, so French, Italian and Spanish loan words in English may be pronounced with / e /.

/ elit /	/ ekru /	/ eklɑ /

For speakers whose first language is French, Italian or Spanish, the "pure" version of this sound is used in places where native speakers of English would use diphthongs. The underlined weak syllable in words such as, ess<u>ay</u> and <u>a</u>political, can be pronounced with the diphthong / eɪ / or the pure vowel / e /.

Write three more words which might use / e /.

SOUND AND MEANING
Exploration: The Energies of the Vowels

Play with each vowel Phonetic-Pillow, allowing the vibrations to move your body as you send the sound through your body. Rub, bounce, stroke your body with each pillow. Play with the sounds divining which parts of your body respond to which vowels. Find out for yourself whether certain vowel sounds seem more attracted to certain places in your body.

Which sounds seem attracted to your legs and feet?

Which sounds are drawn to the middle of your body--your belly?

Which sounds seem to want to move around in your pelvis?

Is there a sound or sounds most at home in your chest--around your heart? your ribcage? spine?

Are there sounds that are more attracted to the back of your body than to the front of your body?

Are there sounds that want to move your arms or your fingers rather than move your torso?

What sounds are more likely to find their home somewhere in your skull?

your mouth?

your cheeks?

your eyes?

your forehead?

the top of your head?

THE RESONATOR SCALE or VOWEL LADDER

Look at the list of vowels below. This configuration is called a *vowel ladder* or *resonator scale*. Begin at the top of the ladder by whispering / i /. Be careful not to whisper in the style of the conventional "stage whisper," in which the breath can be heard as it passes through the throat. Your tongue, jaw and soft palate should feel easy and released. The only sound the breath makes should be in the front of the mouth, between the lips and teeth. The breath flowing through the / i / formation will carry a voiceless pitch with it (something like a pitch heard in the whistle of the wind.) Now go to the bottom of the ladder and whisper / u /. Note that the whispered pitch is much lower. Now whisper through the entire series of vowels one at a time, from / i / to / u /. Whispered in the order indicated below, without audible throat friction, a downward change in pitch can be heard for each successive vowel.

i
ɪ
eɪ
ɛ
æ
ɝ
ʌ
ɑ
ɒ
ɔ
oʊ
ʊ
u

The whispered vowel ladder or resonator scale has been noted and used in speech training by J. Clifford Turner, W.A. Aikin, M.D. and others. The phenomenon is based on the shape of the resonating cavity, determined by the position of jaw, tongue and lips. It is rather scientific, and was once used to "perfect the vowels through their resonant qualities."

It is important that the flow of sound travels unimpeded through the mouth when speaking. A voice which is centered in the throat will not carry the subtle overtones caused by the shape of the mouth opening. You can prove this to yourself by trying a simple experiment. Form the shape of the vowel / u / but don't actually make the sound. While sustaining the / u / shape, gently flick your larynx with a finger just to one side of your Adam's apple. Listen to the pitch which the flick creates within the hollow of your larynx. Now change to the formation of / i /, flick, and again listen for the resultant pitch. Finally, change the shape to / ɑ /, flick and listen for the resultant pitch. Are you surprised to hear that / u / and / i / are nearly the same pitch, and that / ɑ / is much higher? This experiment proves that the inherent "music" of vowels operates differently in the throat than the mouth. To complete this experiment and give it relevance to your voice onstage, whisper the vowel ladder with audible friction in your throat. Do you notice that the whispered pitches don't vary very much? This proves that throat centered speaking removes the intrinsic "music" from the vowels in language. Sigh with relief with no throat friction. Now sigh on your voice with the same throatless feeling. The frictionless sigh is your blueprint for resonant expressive speaking.

Generations of speech students have learned the following mnemonic sentence:

"Who would know aught of art must learn and then take his ease."

Whisper this sentence. Do you hear the successive rise in pitches? Do you hear the individual vowels of the vowel ladder?

Do you hear the differences in the relative lengths of the vowels--the long vowels, the short vowels, the diphthongs?

Traditionally, the attention in speech training was on the acoustics of the mouth and throat to the exclusion of the rest of the body. But in 1989, Kristin Linklater developed a way to use the scale of the vowels to awaken energies in the actor's body. In *Freeing Shakespeare's Voice*, Linklater introduces the vowel scale or vowel ladder as a physical exercise, suggesting that you aim "each sound at a different part of your body" and let each sound "arouse whatever energy, mood, feeling or emotion it wants from you, activating the body into movement as the sound goes through you." (Linklater, Freeing Shakespeare's Voice, p. 23) The exploration can awaken your body, voice and imagination so that the vowels reveal you through the text you are speaking.

Here are the sounds of the vowel ladder to which Linklater has added initial consonants. The consonants in this vowel ladder serve two purposes: 1) they provide the initial fuel to energize each vowel, and 2) they ensure the forward release of sound, enabling each vowel to bypass the throat.

rrri

kɪ

peɪ

dɛ

bæ

hʌ

fə

mɑ

gɒ

ʃɔ

woʊ

zu

Linklater's vowel ladder can be used as a quick warmup: starting at the bottom of the ladder with / u /, work your way upward feeling each successive vowel rise to a higher area of the body and a higher intrinsic pitch. Physicalize each vowel; and, with each new vowel, progress upward in pitch and locate the sound higher in the body.

To embrace this exercise fully requires accurate thinking and vivid imaging. Use the following instructions to locate the vowels in Linklater's vowel ladder as specifically as possible:

/ zu / is a long, low sound which moves through the legs and pelvis.

/ woʊ / is a long, open sound which moves the whole belly area.

/ ʃɔ / another long sound, activate the solar plexus area.

/ gɒ / a dense, short little sound pops out from between the breast bone and the spine, between the shoulder blades.

/ mɑ / is a long, sound releasing from the heart and moving the chest.

/ fə / is a short sound jumping off the chin.

/ hʌ / is a long sound flowing out of the mouth.

/ bæ / is a short sound that springs from the cheeks

/ dɛ / short again, zings from the cheekbones.

/ peɪ / a long sound which radiates vulnerably out from the eyes.

/ kɪ / is a little sound which darts out from the bridge of the nose and almost takes the rest of the body with it.

/ rrri / is a long high sound that jumps out through the top of the skull, causing the body to leave the floor in a little jump.

Draw an outline in the shape of your body. Then draw the phonetic symbols for each vowel on the appropriate part of your body. Let your experience of the vowels moving your body translate onto the page.

Working with the vowel ladder can help you to differentiate vowels from one another, so that each one finds a different home in your body. Knowing that each vowel possesses different inherent musical qualities--a different resonating chamber and a different pitch--may help you to distinguish one vowel's energy from that of another. Just as the physical exploration can aid you in your approach to texts, so can writing the phonetic symbols. You'll learn to take the sounds of a text into your body from the page as you read a text in IPA. Your response to the language on the page will include musical response; almost like musicians who feel the music as they read notes on a score.

Whispering Exercise

Whisper a monologue, free from throat friction, with an awareness of your exploration of the vowel scale. Notice as you move from word to word, vowel to vowel, the whispered pitches change accordingly.

What did you find in your whispered experience?

Now, speak the monologue out loud with awareness of the varied energies of the vowels, being careful not to sing the intrinsic pitches.

Describe your experience of speaking the monologue. What did your awareness of the different vowel energies do for you?

Diphthong Pathway

Each diphthong has the potential for two different "homes" in your body. What pathway through your body would you need to follow to get from the first element of the following diphthongs to the second element? For each of the diphthongs below, draw this body pathway as if it were a diphthong road map.

/ aʊ /

/ ɔɪ /

/ aɪ /

/ eɪ /

/ oʊ /

The Rhythm of the Vowels

You may may have noticed in working with the intrinsic pitches of the vowel ladder, that there are differences in the lengths of the vowels--some tend to be short and some long. Vowels have intrinsic length as well as intrinsic pitch.

Speak the vowels and diphthongs in the vowel ladder below.

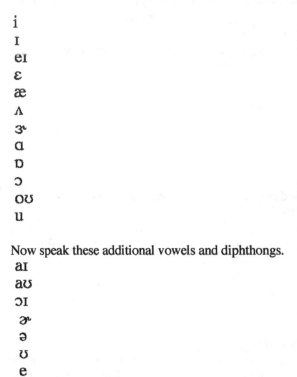

i
ɪ
eɪ
ɛ
æ
ʌ
ɝ
ɑ
ɒ
ɔ
oʊ
u

Now speak these additional vowels and diphthongs.

aɪ
aʊ
ɔɪ
ɚ
ə
ʊ
e
o

All diphthongs are relatively long: / aʊ / , / aɪ /, / ɔɪ /, / eɪ / , / oʊ /. Say these words which contain diphthongs:
how, mime, choice, tame, toast

These vowels are relatively long: / i /, / ɑ /, / ɔ /, / u /. Say these words which contain long vowels:
meal, plaza, bought, tuna

These vowels are relatively short: / ɪ /, / ɛ /, / æ /, / ʌ /, / ə /, / ɒ /, / ʊ /, / ɚ /. Say these words which contain short vowels:
hip, get, bask, fudge, the, what, good, over

Many of the short vowels often occur in weak or unstressed positions within a word or within a sentence. Here are examples of / ɪ /, / ə / and / ɚ / in the weak position of a word:
intent, again, paper.

The relative length of a vowel changes according to its position in a word. Vowels are affected by the sounds around them. Say these words, and note the relative length of the vowels in each.

/ i /   see, eat, feel, brie, peep, scream

/ eɪ /   play, ate, pale, bray, nape, maim

/ æ /   sat, Sam, map, ma'am

/ ɝ /   pearl, furrier, squirrel, purchase

/ ɚ /   urbane, sister, germane

/ ɑ /   father, not   (in words like NOT some people use / ɒ /, some use / ɑ /)

/ u /   school, prove, oops, fruit, soup, spoon

Do you find any relationship between the length of a vowel and its ability to arouse feeling in you?

Try intentionally shortening the longer vowels in the words above. What is the result for you?

Try intentionally lengthening the shorter vowels in words such as "sit, slap, wet, pluck, look."

How does the vowel elongation make you feel about the word?

When words are used in sentences, vowel lengths may change in order to convey meaning. People often alter the intrinsic rhythms of vowels and consonants in the context of conversation. A vowel may increase in length as a means of emphasizing a word. It may decrease in length if the intention of the speaker is to clip the sound, to hide something, to reduce or eliminate feeling from a word. Sometimes speakers intentionally or unintentionally clip all vowels short, reducing their speech to intellectual content only, rather than allowing vowel elongation, which may reveal emotional life. With an awareness of the intrinsic lengths of vowels in a piece of text, you may be able to discover a layer of meaning that a playwright intended through the choice of words. Discovering that a character speaks using predominantly long vowels or predominantly short vowels may point you toward useful choices for speaking the words of the text.

Choose a monologue from a play. Write a one-minute section of the monologue below. Using colored pencils write the phonetic symbols for the vowels above each word. Use the color(s) which evoke feeling and meaning for each individual sound.

CONSONANTS
b

Speak and draw / b /. Color it with colored pencils, crayons or markers. Let your lips come together and explode in vibration, feeling the release of the / b / as you draw and color it. Let it bubble up from behind your lips.

-----Picture yourself as a baby discovering this sound for the first time; playing with it. What might have been three of your first / b / words?

-----Is there anything about the shape of this symbol that could remind you of its sound?

-----Draw three little pictures here, each representing a word that contains / b /.

-----Speak the following nonsense words aloud, allowing the / b / to explode from your lips and open out into the vowel, traveling through your body and out into space.

/ bju /   / bɑ /   / boʊb /   / bɛ /

-----And now speak these multi-syllabic creations.

/ baʊbɔɪ /   / blɑdɪblɑ /   / ɪbibi /   / beɪbə /

51

Draw / p / . Color it with colored pencils, crayons or markers. Let your lips come together and explode, feeling the whispered release of the / p / as you draw and color it. Find the pleasure of the sound; let it play on your lips.

-----Let your fingers speak / p /. Then let your belly speak / p /. Compare the sensations of the two.

-----Is there something pleasurable about the speaking of / p /? How does this phrase feel on your lips: Peter Piper picked a peck of pickled peppers.

d

Speak and draw / d /. Let your tongue touch your gum ridge and explode in vibration, feeling the release of / d / as you draw and color it. Let the sound dally on your tongue as you speak the sound. Delight in the sound.

-----Some researchers say that babies find / d / before they find / m /. Did you say / dædæ / before you said / mɑmɑ / ?

-----Write five silly words that begin with / d /.

-----Write five words that end with / d /.

----- Play all of your / d / words through your body, allowing all of the sounds to express their characters through you. What can you say about the character of / d / ?

t

Draw / t /. Let your tongue touch the upper gum surface behind your teeth and then let the air explode, feeling the release of / t / as you draw and color it. Let it titillate your tongue. Twist and trill the sound in your mouth.

-----Is this sound percussive for you? What instrument could it remind you of?

-----Is there anything about the shape of / t / that could remind you of its sound?

-----Play with the sound on your tongue, teeth and gum ridge. Vary the sound by varying the firmness of the pressure or the placement of your tongue as you read "Scene / t /" from Disciplining Dimes on pages 157-58 in *The Joy of Phonetics and Accents*. Do you prefer a firm / t / or a more delicate / t / ?

-----Speak the following words and feel the response of your breath in your middle:
"Tangy," "tickled," "tease," "tangle," "tryst," "fort," "spirit," "pressed," "dessert." And "battle," "little," "matter," "frittering," "cluster." Is the sound different for you when it is in the middle of a word? How?

Find / g / in your mouth. Draw and color it with colored pencils, crayons or markers. Let your imagination grow and glow.

-----Picture yourself as a baby discovering this sound for the first time, playing with it. Describe the scene.

----Play with different ways of uttering / g /. How would you speak a very light / g /? How would you speak a heavier / g /?

-----Write three words that seem to call for a light / g / and three words that seem to need a heavier / g /.

-----Whisper / g /. What sound does the whispered / g / remind you of?

k

Draw / k /. Let your tongue and soft palate come together and explode, feeling the release of / k / as you draw and color it. Let the sound tickle you.

-----Play with your articulators as you draw this sound. Can you make this sound with different parts of your tongue touching your soft palate? Can you make the sound very light and precise? Can you make it very heavy and sloppy? What does the sound bring out in you?

-----Teachers of comedy have said that / k / is a funny sound. What do you think?

-----Read the following nonsense words containing / k /. Does the sound at the beginning of the word feel different from when it occurs at the end of a word?

/ kiku /   / ɪk /   / æk /   / koʊ /   / ʊk /

/ kɪkɪ /   / kɛkɑ /   / pɪkə /   / teɪkə /

m

Draw and color / m /. Let yourself hum a little tune while you draw the sound.

----Feel the easy / m / vibrations on your lips. Enjoy the vibrations. Describe your associations with this sound.

-----What words come to your mind as you draw / m /? Write five of them here, in IPA.

-----What could you express with the sound / m /? To whom would you express it?

n

"Draw and color / n / . Let your tongue and gum ridge feel and taste the / n / vibrations.

----If this sound were an instrument, what would it be? Why?

-----Think of yourself at age 15. Do you have any associations with this sound from that period in your life?

-----Read "Scene / n /" from "Disciplining Dimes," on page 164 in *The Joy of Phonetics and Accents*. Elongate / n / in each word and taste the sound as you speak it. How does this affect the way the words feel in your mouth and your body?

----Let the sound of / ŋ / massage the middle of your tongue and your soft palate as you draw and color it. Let your imagination sing.

----- Does the sound in isolation remind you of anything? What?

-----This sound can be used with all words that end in "ing," such as "sing," "ring," "bring," "cling;" and words spelled with "ang," such as "hang," "bang." In some accents, speakers say / brɪŋɪn /, / sɪŋɪn / and / seɪɪn /, or / brɪɲin /, / sɪɲin / and / seɪin /, rather than / brɪŋɪŋ /, / sɪŋɪŋ / and / seɪɪŋ /. What is your habitual pronunciation of these words?

_____ _____ _____

Making Connections: More Practice with / b /, / p /, / d /, / t /, / g /, / k /, / m /, / n /, / ŋ /.

Transcribe the following words into IPA. Transcribe each word in what you sense to be the clearest possible pronunciation.

BEAT   / bit /_____   TAPE   _____

FIT   _____   KICK   _____

DOT   _____   TALK   _____

GAG   _____   DOG   _____

BACK   _____   BUG   _____

SKIP   _____   GOOD   _____

RATE   _____   DECK   _____

Translate the following sentences into IPA.

KEEP COMING OUT to TALK to the CAT.

_____tʊ _____tʊ ðə _____.

The NAME of the GAME is "KICK the CAN."

ðə _____əv ðə _____ɪz _____ðə _____.

DON'T BE NICE AT NIGHT, PAY THE SINGER.

_____.

Transcribe the following words into IPA.

NICK   _____   PINE   _____

POKE   _____   NONE   _____

MING   _____   TOWN   _____

SINGING _____   CONE   _____

S

Draw and color / s /. Let the sound snake through your spine, down through your arm and through your fingers, shaping / s /. Let your imagination sail.

-----How does / s / make you feel when you say it?

-----What could you communicate with the sound of / s / ?

-----Play around with different ways of saying / s /. Move your tongue around, move your lips around, lengthen the sound, shorten the sound. What is the most satisfying / s / for you--describe it.

-----In speaking / s /, does the tip of your tongue go slightly upward, toward your top teeth? Or slightly downward, toward your bottom teeth? Which direction results in a clearer, more precise sound? Which is your habit?

Z

Draw / z / . Color it with colored pencils, crayons or markers. Let the sound buzz through your spine, down through your arm and through your fingers, shaping the / z / as you draw and color it. Let your imagination zing.

-----What associations do you have with / z /?

-----Play these / z / words through your body: zealous, dazzling, brazen, cozy, breezy, busy. Let your body take on the character of the / z / as it vibrates through you.

-----Play around with your articulators to achieve the most vibration possible on / z /. What do you have to do to achieve the most vibration?

Draw / f / . Color it with colored pencils, crayons or markers. Let the sound / f / flow through you as you draw and color it. Let your thoughts run free as you let the sound flow through you onto the page.

-----What kind of a character would the / f / be in a Restoration comedy? Fluffy? swift? miffed? frightened? flimsy? feisty? fickle? fitful? fried? Would he/she want to fight? flee? feast?

-----Write a short monologue for your / f / character, using plenty of / f /.

Draw and color / v / . Savor the sound, move the sound down through your arm and through your fingers, shaping the / v / as you draw and color it. Let your imagination revive.

-----What associations do you have with / v /?

-----Speak these words aloud, moving them through your body:

vivacious, vibrant, savvy, voracious, vigilant, vibrate, vacillate, vilify, or vivisect.

Feel the vibrations between your top teeth and bottom lip. Vary the pressure and be aware of the change in the feeling of vibrations. What do you notice?

Speak Sonnet 63 aloud with an awareness of / v /.

Against my love shall be as I am now,
With Time's injurious hand crushed and o'erworn;
When hours have drained his blood and filled his brow
With lines and wrinkles, when his youthful morn
Hath traveled on to Age's steepy night,
And all those beauties whereof now he's king
Are vanishing, or vanished out of sight,
Stealing away the treasure of his spring;
For such a time do I now fortify
Against confounding Age's cruel knife,
That he shall never cut from memory
My sweet love's beauty, though my lover's life.
  His beauty shall in these black lines be seen
  And they shall live, and he in them still green.

Write the words in Sonnet 63 which contain the sound / v / :

_____ _____ _____ _____ _____ _____

_____ _____ _____ _____

Draw / ʃ / . Shimmy the sound; shake the sound down through your arm and through your fingers, shaping / ʃ / as you draw and color it.

-----Where does / ʃ / seem to want to go in your body? See if you can move it around to other places in your body, awakening them with this whispered sound.

----- Speak these words from the Sonnets aloud with an awareness of / ʃ /.
Write the words in IPA here:

SHADOWS_____

GRECIAN_____

SPECIAL_____

SHARP_____

FLESH_____

PRECIOUS_____

SHIFTING_____

SHOULD_____

3

Speak and draw / ʒ / . Color it with colored pencils, crayons or markers. Take pleasure in the sound as you let it flow leisurely down through your arm and through your fingers, shaping / ʒ / as you draw and color it.

-----What associations do you have with / ʒ /? Feel the buzz of vibrations between your tongue and gum ridge. Where else in your body do you feel vibrations?

-----Vary the pressure of the / ʒ / and be aware of the change in the feeling of vibrations. What do you notice?

-----Write words that begin with / ʒ / here. These may include foreign words:

_____   _____

-----Write words that end with / ʒ / here:

_____   _____

-----Write words that contain / ʒ / in the middle here:

_____   _____

Speak and draw / θ / . Color it with colored pencils, crayons or markers. Think the sound down through the middle of your body, whispering / θ / as you draw and color it. Let your imagination thrill to the thought.

-----Where is your tongue when you speak / θ /? Experiment with the position of your tongue in relation to your teeth.

-----How does the sound engage your breath? Your mouth?

-----Can you feel the breath between your tongue and your teeth?

Speak these words from the Sonnets aloud with an awareness of / θ /. Compare your pronunciations with those indicated in IPA. If your pronounciation is different than the printed transcription write it in the blank to the right.

DOTH	/ dʌθ /	_____
POSSESSETH	/ pəzɛsəθ /	_____
METHINKS	/ miθɪŋks /	_____
HATH	/ hæθ /	_____
STRENGTH	/ strɛŋθ /	_____
TRUTH	/ truθ /	_____
WEALTH	/ wɛlθ /	_____
EARTH	/ ɝθ /	_____

Speak the vibrations of / ð / . Draw the symbol and color it with colored pencils, crayons or markers. Slather the sound down through your arm and through your fingers, shaping / ð / as you draw and color it. Let your imagination bathe in the sound.

----- Feel the vibrations between your tongue and teeth. Vary the pressure of / ð / and be aware of the change in the feeling of vibrations.

-----Is there anything about the shape of the symbol that can help you to remember this sound? Find something and describe it here.

Transcribe the following words into IPA. Speak the words as you write the IPA transcription of your pronunciation. Let the words use your body. Compare your body sensations of / θ / (right) with your sensations of / ð / (left).

BATHE _____   BATH _____

LATHER _____   PATH _____

THEY _____   THIGH _____

THE _____   THINK _____

RATHER_____   PATHWAY_____

-----Sing a tune on / ð /. It is a singable sound because it can be voiced on different pitches; a melody can be sung on the vibrations of / ð /. What other consonants are singable?

Fricative Action: (frɪ kə tɪv) sounds which are caused by friction occuring between two articulating surfaces are known as "fricative" sounds. In English, the fricative consonants are: / f /, / v /, / s /, / z /, / θ /, / ð /, / ʃ /, and / ʒ /.

/ v / and / f /

-----Voice / v / feeling vibrations gather on your bottom lip. Notice where else you feel vibrations--on your top teeth? in the bones in the front of your face? in your skull? in your chest? in your middle? in your legs? Where?

-----Vary the pitch of / v / and see if the feeling of vibrations changes. How is your experience of / v / different on high pitches from your experience on low pitches?

-----Whisper / v /, without thinking about the resulting sound. Let it surprise you. You will probably arrive at something like / f /. Discover how / f / is different from / v /. What shift do you find happens in your thought? Is there any shift in the images that occur to you?

-----Is there any shift in the "position" of your lips and teeth between / v / and / f / ?

-----Shift back and forth between / v / and / f / without changing the position of your articulators. Is your experience of either of the sounds shifted through this awareness?

-----Speak the following words from the Sonnets, feeling the vibrations of / v /.

| LOVE | GRAVE | LEAVE | VILE | THRIVERS | SERVING |

-----Speak the following / f / words; compare them to the / v / words above.

| LAUGH | GRAPH | LEAF | FILE | RIFE | SURF |

/ z / and / s /

-----Speak / z / feeling vibrations gather in the front of your mouth. Notice where you feel vibrations--on your top teeth? in your gum ridge? in the bones in the front of your face? in your skull? in your chest? in your middle? in your legs? Where?

-----Whisper / z /, without thinking about the resulting sound. Let it surprise you. You will probably arrive at something like / s /. How is / s / different from / z / for you? What shift do you find happens in your thought?

-----Is there any shift in the "position" of your tongue?

-----Shift back and forth between / z / and / s / without changing the position of your articulators. Is your experience of either of the sounds shifted through this awareness?

-----Some speakers speak / s / or a partially devoiced / z / in the plural forms of the words below. Speak the following words from the Sonnets, and commit to the full vibrations of / z /.

EYES   WEEDS   FLOWERS   SLANDERERS   CROSSES

STANDS   SICKLE'S   SEEMS   SCHEMES   MAZES

-----Speak the following words, fully commiting to / s /.

PRINTS   PROPS   APPETITES   FAULTS   BATHS   BLANKS

-----Now that you have contrasted / z / and / s / notice how each feels in your mouth. Write a "rule" for the difference between using / z / and / s / for plural forms of words.

-----Apply this same rule to possessive forms such as: Ruth's, Ed's, Flo's, Buzz's and Chris's.

-----Apply the same rule to third person singular forms of the following verbs: goes, thinks, runs, passes, fizzes.

/θ/ and /ð/

-----Voice / ð / feeling vibrations gather in the front of your mouth. Notice where you feel vibrations-- are they between your teeth? in your gum ridge? in the bones in the front of your face? in your skull? in your chest? in your middle? in your legs? Vary the pressure and see if your awareness of vibration changes. Vary the pitch and see if your experience changes.

-----Whisper / ð /, without thinking about the resulting sound. Let it surprise you. You will probably arrive at the sound / θ /. Discover how / θ / is different from / ð /. What shift do you find happens in your thought? Is there any shift in the images that occur to you? Is there any shift in the "position" of your tongue?

-----Speak Sonnet 37, feeling the vibrations of / ð / contrasted with the whispered experience of / θ /.

As a decrepit father takes delight
To see his active child do deeds of youth,
So I, made lame by Fortune's dearest spite,
Take all my comfort of thy worth and truth.
For whether beauty, birth, or wealth, or wit,
Or any of these all, or all, or more,
Entitled in their parts do crowned sit,
I make my love engrafted to this store.
So then I am not lame, poor, nor despised
Whilst that this shadow doth such substance give
That I in thy abundance am sufficed
And by a part of all thy glory live.
  Look what is best, that best I wish in thee.
  This wish I have, then ten times happy me.

Write the words in this sonnet containing / ð / and / θ / in IPA below.

_____   _____   _____   _____

_____   _____   _____   _____

_____   _____   _____   _____

_____   _____   _____   _____

Transcribe the following words into IPA:

FAVOR_____   VIGOROUS _____

SANGUINE _____   ZITHER _____

THINKING _____   VISUAL _____

ISSUE   _____   TREASURY _____

Translate the following sentences to English Spelling.

/ ðə fækt ðæt mæn kəmjunɪkeɪts wɪθ hɪz hoʊl bɑdi θru ɔl hɪz sɛnsɪz ɪz ɛvɪdənt tʊ ʌs tʊdeɪ mɑdɚn saɪkɑlədʒi hæz ʌndɚskɔrd ðə weɪ ɪn wɪtʃ ðə tʃaɪld kənstrʌkts hɪz fɝst wɝld ʌndɚ ði ɪnflʊəns əv tʌtʃ əv teɪst ænd əv smɛl æz wɛl əz əv saʊnd ænd saɪt   saʊnd ə midiəm əv kəmjunɪkeɪʃn sɪns ðə tʃaɪldz fɝst kraɪ mænɪfɛsts nu pətɛnʃl əv minɪŋ æz ðə tʃaɪld pæsɪz θru ðə lɑlɪŋ steɪdʒ   ðə prɛzəns əv ðə wɝd baɪ wɔltɚ ɔŋ /

_____

_____

_____

_____

_____

_____

/ naʊ ju kæn rid ɪn aɪ pi eɪ /

Whisper and draw / ʧ /. Color it with colored pencils, crayons or markers. Chomp on the sound; pitch the sound down through your arm and through your fingers, churning the / ʧ / as you draw and color it. Let your imagination cheer.

-----What associations do you have with / ʧ /?

-----Write a sentence here (in IPA) that contains four or five words which you pronounce with / ʧ /.

_____

_____

/ ʧ / combines the plosive / t / and the frictioned, continued sound of / ʃ /. Speak these two sounds separately a few times and then combine them into / ʧ /. A combination of a plosive and affricative is called an affricate. There are two affricates in English / ʧ / and / ʤ /.

----- Speak these words from the Sonnets aloud with an awareness of / ʧ /.
Write the words in IPA here:

FORTUNE_____

TEACHEST_____

CHIEF_____

WATCHMAN_____

CHOPPED_____

FILCHING_____

CHILDREN_____

CHEEKS_____

Find the vibrations of / ʤ / . Draw and color it with colored pencils, crayons or markers. Let / ʤ / take a gentle journey through your body.

-----What associations do you have with / ʤ /? Does it make you feel jealous? jittery? ingenuous? fragile? incorrigible? adjusted? magical? logical? allergic? Do you want to joke? jump? jive? gesture? jingle? adjudicate? adjourn? conjure? legislate? Speak those words aloud, moving them through your body. Feel the vibrations between your tongue and gum ridge.

-----Where else in your body do you feel vibrations?

/ ʤ / combines the plosive / d / with the frictioned, continued sound of / ʒ /. Speak those sounds separately a few times, being aware of their affects on you. Imagine yourself inventing the / ʤ / to serve some purpose, to express some feeling or thought. Is / ʤ / a wholly distinct sound for you or does it express a combination of / d / and / ʒ /? A plosive sound combined with a fricative sound is called an affricate. There are two affricates in English / ʧ / and / ʤ /.

Speak these words from Sonnets aloud with an awareness of / ʤ /. Transcribe each word into IPA.

AGE_____

MARJORAM_____

GENERAL_____

ENJOYER_____

JEWEL_____

ENLARGED_____

ADVANTAGE_____

1

Draw / l / . Color it with colored pencils, crayons or markers. Linger over the sound as it flows leisurely down through your arm and through your fingers, shaping / l / as you draw and color it.

-----What affect do these words have on you?

      whirl, swirl, dally, wallow, follow, linger or twinkle

Speak those words aloud, moving them through your body. Feel the response of your tongue to the thought of / l /.

----- Speak: "light," "live," "large," and "lackey" and then: "unfurl," "sensual," "pale," and "quill."
Does the sound feel different to you when it is at the beginning of the word than it does when it is at the end? Some people find their tongues in a different place for the formation of / l / depending on its placement in the word. Is your tongue performing the same action in all of these words--or does it form / l / differently depending on the context?

-----In isolation, the / l / might almost feel like a vowel to you if you sing it or sustain it. Sing this song transcribed below using the words, then sing just the tune on a sustained / l /.

/ sʌm seɪ lʌv ɪt ɪz ə rɪvɚ ðæt drɑʊnz ðə tɛndɚ rid sʌm seɪ lʌv ɪt ɪz ə reɪzɚ ðæt lidz ðə soʊl tu

blid sʌm seɪ lʌv ɪt ɪz ə hʌŋgɚ æn ɛndləs eɪkɪŋ nid aɪ seɪ lʌv ɪt ɪz ə flaʊr ænd ju ði oʊnli sid /

-----Describe / l /'s personality as if it were a person.

Find / w / on your lips. Draw and color it with colored pencils, crayons or markers. Watch the sound wind through your body, down through your arm and through your fingers, shaping / w / as you draw and color it. Let your imagination take wing as you let the sound waft through you onto the page.

-----Does the sound make you feel wistful? wishful? warlike? wavy? suave? sweet? woozy? Do you want to whistle? wangle? waffle? weigh? Do you want to whirl? wallow? wink? twinkle? Speak these / w / words aloud, moving them through your body. Feel the response of your lips to the thought of / w /.

-----If you sustain the / w /, what vowel do you sound?

-----/ w / is a sound whose character isn't fully realized until you release it into the vowel sound which follows it. Its chameleon-like character releases as it glides into the next sound.

Speak this passage from Sonnet 90 aloud with an awareness of / w /.

/ðɛn heɪt mi ɪf ðaʊ wɪlt ɪf ɛvɚ naʊ

naʊ hwaɪl ðə wɚld ɪz bɛnt maɪ didz tʊ krɔs

dʒɔɪn wɪð mi ðə spaɪt əv fɔrtʃən meɪk mi baʊ

ænd du nɑt drɑp ɪn fɔr ən æftɚlɔs

aɪ dʊ nɑt, hwɛn maɪ hɑrt hæθ skeɪpt ðɪs sɑro,

kʌm ɪn ðə rɪrwɚd əv ə kɑŋkɚd woʊ

gɪv nɑt ə wɪndɪ naɪt ə reɪnɪ mɑroʊ

tʊ lɪŋgɚ aʊt ə pɚpəst oʊvɚθroʊ

ɪf ðaʊ wɪlt liv mi dʊ nɑt liv mi læst,

hwɛn ʌðɚ pɛtɪ grifs hæv dʌn ðɛr spaɪt

bət ɪn ði ɑnsɛt kʌm soʊ ʃæl aɪ teɪst

æt fɚst ðə vɛrɪ wɚst əv fɔrtʃənz maɪt

  ænd ʌðɚ streɪnz əv woʊ wɪtʃ naʊ sim woʊ

  kəmpɛrd wɪθ lɔs əv ði wɪl nɑt sim soʊ /

There are words in the sonnet that are spelled with "w" but do not contain / w / as a sound. What are those words?

_____   _____   _____   _____

_____

hw

Whisper and draw / hw / . Color it with colored pencils, crayons or markers. Let the sound whet your appetite, shaping the / hw / as you draw and color it. On a whim, let it whoosh through you onto the page.

-----What associations do you have with / hw /? Does it make you feel like whistling? Feel the response of your lips to the thought of / hw /.

Do you use / hw / in your accent? It is seldom used these days. Whom do you know that uses the sound?

Write a sentence here (in IPA) that contains four or five words which could be pronounced with / hw /.

_____

_____

-----/ hw / is one of the sounds whose character isn't fully realized until you release it into the vowel sound that follows it.

-----Imagine that the / hw / and / w / sounds are living, breathing creatures. How is the character of / hw / different from / w / ?

-----Speak this passage from Sonnet 121 aloud with / hw /.

"For why should others' false adulterate eyes

Give salutation to my sportive blood?

Or on my frailties why are frailer spies,

Which in their wills count bad what I think good?"

-----What different meaning or feeling is revealed to you as you speak text with / hw /?

h

Feel your breath as you whisper / h / . Draw and color it with colored pencils, crayons or markers. Give the sound a home in your mouth and in your body as you whisper it. Let it hasten through your head and through your heart, shaping / h / on the page as you draw and color it.

-----What associations do you have with / h / ? Does it make you feel hasty? horrible? hellbent? hip? Do you want to hiccup? holler? heave? Speak these / h / words aloud, moving them through your body.

-----/ h / is a sound whose character isn't fully realized until you release it into the vowel sound that follows it. What does it feel like to you in isolation?

Speak Sonnet 120 aloud with an awareness of / h /. Write the words containing / h / in IPA to the right of the selection below.

"That you were once unkind befriends me now,

And for that sorrow which I then did feel

Needs must I under my transgression bow,

Unless my nerves were brass or hammered steel.   _____

For if you were by my unkindness shaken,

As I by yours, Y'have passed a hell of time,   _____

And I, a tyrant, have no leisure taken

To weigh how once I suffered in your crime.   _____

O, That our night of woe might have rememb'red

My deepest sense how hard true sorrow hits,   _____

And soon to you, as you to me then, tend'red

The humble salve which wounded bosoms fits?   _____

　　But that your trespass now becomes a fee;

　　Mine ransoms yours, and yours must ransom me.

What feeling is revealed to you, as you speak with your attention on the sound / h / ?

j

Draw / j /. Color it with colored pencils, crayons or markers. Yawl the sound and then lie back and yawn. Feel the response of your tongue to the thought of / j /.

-----What associations do you have with / j /?

-----/ j / might almost feel like a vowel to you if you sing it or sustain it without releasing it. But, its true character is released as it glides into the next sound. What vowel might you get if you sustained / j /?

Write a short story about yourself as a youth. Make sure it has a beginning, middle, and end. Write in IPA only the words in the story containing / j /. Use the sound / j / in as many words as possible.

Consonant Journeys: Practice for / dʒ /, /tʃ /, / l /, / w /, / hw / and / j /.

The combination symbol / ju / is used to indicate the vowel combination called the "liquid u" or the "long u." Do you use / ju / or / u / in each of the following words? Write the symbol for the sound you use below.

/ ju / or / u / ?

_____USUAL

_____NEWS

_____STUDENT

_____NUDE

_____ILLUSION

Speak this speech from "Disciplining Dimes" (on page 140 of *The Joy of Phonetics and Accents*) in IPA using your own accent. Then speak it using / ju / for every capitalized word. Then speak it again using your own accent; being aware of the differences, if there are any.

"That old COSTUME. An ILLUSION played out on CUE with every DUPE, every TUNIC ready to burst buttons. And the tuxedo blistering my chest, my chest mind YOU, with only a penguin to RESUME the DUTIFUL ice CUBE dance."

Speak the following phrases, from the Sonnets, comparing the sounds of / ju / and / u /. Speak them using first one sound, then the other. Do you have a preference? If so, is it an aesthetic preference?

Sonnet 129 "Mad in pursuit, and in possession so."

Sonnet 102 "Our love was new, and then but in the spring,"

Sonnet 94 "Others but stewards of their excellence."

Sonnet 22 "Presume not on the heart when mine is slain;
        Thou gav'st me thine, not to give back again."

You may be more accustomed to using / ju / than / u / in certain words. Compare the two sounds in the following words from the Sonnets. For which words do you use / ju / ?

BEAUTY, MUSE, YOUTH, YOU, ABUSE, UNUSED, PURSUIT, NEW, STEWARDS, PRESUME

r

Revel in the consonant / r / as you sound it. Draw and color it with colored pencils, crayons or markers. Roll the sound around in your mouth. Let it resonate and reverberate through your body.

-----What associations do you have with / r / ?

Write the following words in IPA below.

raunchy, rustic, risky, rank, rally, roam, aroused, brash, thrashed, erased, berated, crazy

_____   _____   _____

_____   _____   _____

_____   _____   _____

_____   _____   _____

Write a poem of your own below, using the consonant / r / as much as possible. Write two stanzas of four lines each. Put some rhythm and rhyme in your poem.

Vowels of "r"

In one syllable words, such as "rose" and "corn," there is no question as to which syllable is accented--the vowel is therefore in a strong position. But what happens when we find a vowel in relationship to r in a weak (or unaccented) syllable of a word, such as in "mother?" Say the word "mother" and notice the way you handle the final r sound. Is it a very "hard r" sound? medium? dropped? soft?

The weak-syllable vowel is usually represented as / ɚ / or / ə /.

MOTHER   / mʌðɚ / or / mʌðə /

Here is a variation: / ər /. How is it different?

MOTHER   / mʌðər /

Transcribe the following words, in your own accent, using one of the three choices for the weak syllable of the "er" vowel:

SUPPER_____

FLAPPER_____

BEAKER_____

Consider the vowel "r" in the word "bird." Because "bird" is a one-syllable word, its only vowel is in an accented position. It is inaccurate to transcribe the vowel in "bird" as / ɚ /, / ə / or / ər / because they are reserved for the transcription of neutral vowels in unaccented syllables. For accented syllables, you will need a different vowel symbol. The accented symbol can be transcribed in two different ways: with an "r-tail" / ɝ / and without an "r-tail" / ɜ /. When transcribed with an "r-tail" (indicating r-coloring) it represents a common North American pronunciation of the vowel. When transcribed without the "r-tail," it represents a common Southern British pronunciation of the vowel. Not everyone in a given region pronounces "er" in the same way, but both of these are common in their own regions.

With a partner, read scene / ɝ / from "The Undiapered Filefish" (on page 132 of *The Joy of Phonetics*.) Make sure that you are using the vowel / ɝ / in every case, even if you do not typically do this in your own accent. How does it feel to read the scene in this way?

Now read the scene again using the vowel / ɜ / in place of / ɝ /. If you are not familiar with this sound, you may need your teacher, or a Southern British native to make the sound clear to you. Be aware that it is not just /ə/ switched to the accented position of a word. If it were, the symbol / ʌ / would be used. Notice changes in your attitude, physicality, energy and imagination which take place as you use the / ɜ / sound. What do you find?

Revel in RRRRRRRRR: More Practice with the Consonant / r / and the Vowels / ɝ / and / ɚ /

Spoken in isolation, the following three sounds, the consonant / r /, and the two r-colored vowels, / ɝ / and / ɚ / might sound exactly the same. How are they different? Or, why are they different? Why distinguish between them at all? An "r" is an "r" is an "r," you might say. Read the following words and see if you can come to some conclusions about how the consonant / r / is used and how the vowels / ɝ / and / ɚ / are used.

/ reɪk /   / raʊz /   / roʊ /   / rili /   / rizn /   / əraʊzɪŋ /   / əraʊnd /   / sɝtʃ /   / fɝst /   / hɝd /
/ grɪp /   / friz /   / zɪpɚ /   / pɚtɝb /

Conclusions?

R is a meaningful sound. Sometimes when you are angry or upset, you might say "errrrrrrrrrr." Sometimes you might say "er" when you can't think of what to say next, or when you're put on the spot. These are significant human utterances. Beyond words. In place of words. Filling in for words.

Some cultures and regions embrace r fully--Southwestern US and Ireland, for instance. Some places have an r all their own--like France or Scotland. Some cultures shun the r as if it were unworthy, Southern England, most notably. Don't let anyone talk you out of the sound of your r. If it is a somewhat guttural or throaty sound, as some claim, then you must be able to transition between it and more forward sounds quickly and nimbly. But eradicate it in the name of good speech???? errrrrrrr!!! Your r is your birthright.

Students often get confused about the myriad ways in which r is expressed phonetically.
Speak the sounds represented by the symbols below:

r   ɚ   ɝ   ɜ   ə

/ r /

For native speakers of English, / r / is the sound at the beginning of a word such as ROSE. It is also the sound in the middle of a word, between two vowels, such as VERY. It is also the sound before a consonant in the speech of people who do not drop their r's, in words such as PARK and SHORT. It is also the sound at the end of a word for people who do not drop their r's, in words, such as FLOOR, and CAR.

There are many varying pronunciations of / r /. Have you heard the term "hard r ?" Think of the speech of a Texan. Think of the speech of a person from Northern Ireland. Compare it to the speech of someone who drops some or all of their r's, such as a New Yorker, a Londoner, or a Bostonian. With your mind's ear, can you hear the difference? Can you feel the difference when your tongue pulls further back in your mouth? Whom do you know who uses a "hard r ?"

Consonant / r / and vowels of "r"

Even people who are "heavy r users" tend to use "r" differently in different parts of a word. Say these four words and see how the capricious "r" may behave differently in each:

rose   corn   mother   bird

Use these words in a sentence, make them about something--pour yourself into it. "Mother rose with the birds and made cornbread." Invent a different sentence using these four words.

Does your "r" pronounciation change its nuance in these different words?

Is the r "harder" in one of the words?

Is the r shorter in one of the words?

Now read the words, written phonetically:

/ roʊz /   / kɔrn /   / mʌðɚ /   / bɝd /

Which of these transcriptions matches your own speech?

For some people, the r is an extra-hard sound. If that's who you are, you can intensify the r in transcription, by putting a nuance mark beneath it. If you put a minus sign under the r like this, / r̠ / it indicates that the tongue is pulled back further than it would be for a medium-strength / r /.

/ r̠oʊz /

If your r derives its intensity from elongation, you can express this by putting a colon after it:

/ rːoʊz /

If you were to tap your "r" on your gum ridge (as in Spanish accents) you might use a small r above the line:

/ ˼oʊz /

If you were to trill your "r" at the back of your throat, producing a uvular French "r," you might use one or several small r's above the line:

/ ˼˼˼oʊz /

Beginning r's are usually quite distinct, even in the speech of people who drop final and presonsonant r's. After all, if you were to drop the r from "rose," all you would have left would be "ose." In some accents however, you will hear a lighter form of initial r than is commonly heard among native speakers of English. In German accents the r can be very breathy, almost sounding like an h. In Japanese accents, an r can sound like an l or a mixture of r and l. Some people who have trouble saying r pronounce it like w.

Using the / r / diphthongs
Let's look at the many roles "r" can play in relationship to other sounds. Some people say / kɔrn /, others say / kɔɪn /, others say / koɚn / and still others say / koən /, to name just a few common pronunciations for the word "corn." Which one is closest to your speech? (If yours is different from any of these, write the phonetic transcription of your pronunciation.)

In some dictionaries, words like corn are transcribed like this: / kɔɚn /.

The following is a demonstration of different transcription styles for diphthongs of "r." Note the variations in pronunciation and IPA spellings:

HEAR	hɪr	hir	hɪɚ	hɪə	
HAIR	hɛr	heɪr	hɛɚ	hɛə	
HARSH	hɑrʃ	hɑɪʃ			
HORSE	hɔrs	hors	hoɚs	hɔɪs	
POOR	pʊr	pur	pʊɚ	pʊə	puɚ

Read the following words and notice what type of "r" you use when you say them. Transcribe your pronunciations here:

EAR_____   FIRE_____

AIR_____   FLOUR_____

ARE_____   LAWYER_____

OR_____

POOR_____

IPA Pillow Games for "r"

Stand in a circle with the word "stir" / stɝ / spelled out in Phonetic Pillows on the floor in the center. Now pick up the / ɝ / pillow and begin tossing it from person to person while saying the word "stir." Make sure your pronunciation of "stir" is faithful to the transcription which was spelled out on the floor. As you toss the pillow, you have the opportunity to explore the sound physically as well as vocally. Involve your entire body in sending the word and pillow across the circle. Desire to communicate the meaning of the word through the gesture of its sounds.

After this pronunciation of the word "stir" has been explored by each member of the group, switch from tossing the / ɝ / pillow to the / ɜ / pillow. As before, continue to say the word "stir" as you toss the pillow, involving your entire body. But now pronounce "stir" according to this new transcription. Notice any changes as you toss this new sound around. What feels different in your body?   Where does your imagination take you? What choices occur to you which are different from before?

After you have explored the two versions of this sound individually, continue the game with both / ɜ / and / ɝ / being tossed by different players at the same time. Make sure to be true to the sound of the pillow you receive, and to fully embody it. Be very interested in the psycho-physical differences that each of these sounds evokes in you. After you have tossed the word "stir" using these two sounds for a while, add the sound / ʌ / to the game. What is your response to this new substitution? Do you get a different image? A different feeling?

Now play another round of this game with the word "cover" / kʌvɚ / spelled out in Phonetic Pillows on the floor in the middle of the circle. As before, begin by tossing the / ɚ / pillow while saying the word "cover," being true to the pronunciation of the pillow in play. Involve your whole body and notice how this particular sound influences and fuels you emotionally, physically, imaginatively and mentally. Feel the gesture of the word in your body and let the meaning be sent through it.

Now switch to the / ə / pillow. As you toss this sound feel the difference caused by the absence of " r."

After you have tossed / ə / for a while, switch to the / r / pillow. As you toss it, feel how this abundance of "r" at the end of the word "cover" causes different associations and sensations for you. What did you find?

"r" Diphthong Pillow Game

The group forms a circle and places the / ɪ / pillow on the floor in the center. Each member of the group then tosses the / ɚ / pillow while making its sound in combination with the pillow on the floor, in a series which begins with / ɪ / and ends with / ɚ /. The resultant sound, / ɪɚ / is known as an "r diphthong." After the group has tossed this "r" diphthong sound around for awhile, switch from tossing the / ɚ / pillow to tossing the / r / pillow. Notice the difference in the resultant sound combination. The sound / ɪr / does not have the transitional vowel sound of the schwa with which to ease into the / r / the way the sound / ɪɚ / does. Compare these two styles of "r" diphthongs. Which is closer to your pronunciation of the word "ear?"

How many other ways are there to say "ear?" Try another round of this game, substituting the / ɪ / pillow on the floor with the / i / pillow. Use this as the initial vowel in the "r diphthong" as you first toss / ɚ / and then / r / around the circle. Is this version of "ear " more familiar to you?

Now turn to pages 23-27 in *The Joy of Phonetics* and continue playing the "r" diphthong game using / r / in combination with other vowels and diphthongs.

All of the "r" games should be played often, using many different words. This is the beginning of assimilating new accents through a psycho-physical process. You can explore the differences between American and British accents or those of different regions of the U.S. Try these games with a comparison of Southwestern U.S. and New England accents, for instance. If you make it a given of the exercise that the r pillow represents the uvular trill, you can begin to learn a French accent. If you endow the "r" pillow with an intensely rhotic quality, you can begin to explore a Northern Irish accent. As you get more familiar with the game, you can move beyond substitutions merely involving the different qualities of "r." You can play these games using any vowel or consonant substitutions.

"r" in the middle of a word

Knowing which form of "r" to use in transcription can be a confusing matter. The rule of thumb should be to use the form which most closely resembles the sound and style of the speaker whose accent you are transcribing. However, here is some useful information to keep in mind when there is an "r" sound at the beginning or end of a syllable: in a word such as "clearly," it is obvious that the syllable division takes place between the r and the l. This word could be transcribed with either the schwa plus r-tail symbol, / klɪɚ li /, the schwa followed by an r, / klɪər li / or, for a harder r, the vowel / ɪ / followed by r, / klɪr li /. However, in a word such as "clearance," if the first syllable ends in r, the second must begin with a vowel. This could easily result in a throat-centred second syllable, because a syllable beginning with a vowel is likely to cause glottal shock. Here is a transcription of the word clearance in which the first syllable ends with an r sound and the second syllable begins with a glottalized vowel, / klɪɚ ʔəns /. (The symbol / ʔ / indicates a "glottal stop." See page 146 for information about nuance markings. Now, here is a transcription of the same word in which the second syllable begins with r rather than a vowel, and glottal shock is avoided: / klɪ rəns /.

Speak the following words in such a way that the first syllable ends in an / ɚ /, and the second syllable begins with a glottalized vowel. Then say these words in such a way that the second syllable begins with / r /, and glottal shock is avoided. Notice which of these two ways of speaking is closer to your own speaking style. Transcribe the words in your own style.

BARREL_____ CARRIER_____

PARROT_____ ARROW_____

Foreign-accent Uses of R

Different accents use many different pronunciations of the consonant / r /. It can be tapped, trilled, devoiced, rhotacized or retracted or retroflexed, murmured, frictionless, uvular or rolled. Some accents use an "intrusive r." Some eliminate "r coloring" for vowel sounds; some emphasize and lengthen the "hard r. " The way you use the consonant / r / in its various vowel versions says a lot about you-- and can say a lot about the character you portray.

Jerry Blunt, in *Stage Dialects*, calls the / r / the "most versatile of all vocal sounds." Blunt says, "it is slurred or dropped in American Southern, Japanese, and Standard English; hardened in Midwestern American and Irish; single tapped in Standard English, Japanese, and others; trilled with tip of tongue in Scottish, Russian, and Italian; trilled with back of tongue and uvula in French and German; and changed to a half or a full / l / in Japanese."

There is a version of the "r" in Czech where the sound is called the "voiced, strident apico-alveolar fricative trill" according to the *Phonetic Symbol Guide* by Pullum and Ladusaw. According to the same source, there is a symbol used for a "voiced alveolar lateral flap" which is between / l / and / d /, and is used in Tswana.

Be alert to different ways you hear people speaking / r /. Whom do you know that pronounces the sound differently from the way you do? How is it different?

The Tap-trilled "r"

The use of "r" in a British accent is often different from that of most American accents. For an outline of these differences, see pages 117-18 in *The Joy of Phonetics*. It is no longer usual to tap-trill an "r" in British RP speech. For an explanation of British RP speech, see *The Joy of Phonetics*, pages 112-116. However, if you are doing a period play that requires a British accent, it is sometimes useful to include this sound. To hear this sound authentically used by a donor, you will probably have to find a recording of a British performer from the first half of the twentieth century. To make a tap trill, put the tip of your tongue on the gum ridge, in the general position of a / d /, and lightly flip the tongue downward. Your teacher can guide you toward the formation of this sound, but it might take some practice to get it just right. Say these words using a tap-trilled "r," noticing what influence this sound has on you: "very," "sorry," "serious," "experiment." An "r" can also be tap-trilled between words in cases where a word ending with "r" is followed by a word which begins with a vowel, such as "there is," "are in," "you're only," and "before I." Practice the r tap in these phrases.

R-Linking

In phrases like "there is," "are in," "you're only," and "before I," many people link the final "r" onto the vowel which begins the next word. Such an r-link can be transcribed as / ðɛə rɪz /. For more information on r-linking see page 117 of *The Joy of Phonetics and Accents*.

The Trilled or Burred "r"

In Scots, the "r" is often trilled; the trill sound is just like the tap-trilled sound but it is produced in a multiple stream. It is transcribed with two or more small "r"s in a row. A Scots transcription of the word "rose" might be / ʀoɪz / or / ʀʀʀoɪz /. The very energetic Scottish trill is known as a "burr." Some people find they can do the burred "r" quite easily; for others it requires practice. Listen to native speakers.

The French r

If you work with a French accent donor (see page 83 of *The Joy of Phonetics*) you will be struck by the dramatic difference between the French and the American "r." The French "r" is made in the back of the mouth by trilling the uvula against the back of the tongue. The resultant friction-filled sound is known as a uvular trill. In a French accent, the word "rose" could be transcribed as / ʀ oz /. Your teacher may be able to guide you toward making this sound, but nothing beats the first-hand experience of hearing a native speaker or "donor." If you don't get it right away, don't be discouraged; be persistent. Convince your body that it is possible to communicate with this sound. Convince your tongue and uvula that they can work together in this way.

Once you have the knack of the French "r," read scene / r / in "The Undiapered Filefish" (on page 140 of *The Joy of Phonetics*) using the French "r." Also read scenes / ɝ / and / ɚ / (on pages 131 and 132) in this way. Then reexperience the pillow game above using the French "r" sound. Another way of transcribing the uvular "r" is / ʀ /.

The German r

In a German accent, "r" is clearly trilled, except at the end of a word when it is sometimes reduced to a single tap of the tongue. Having explored the French "r", now explore the somewhat different quality of a German "r" (see page 83 in *The Joy of Phonetics*.) The German "r" can have a breathy, aspirated quality Find a German donor to assist you in making an accurate German sound. Read the German scenes from "The Undiapered Filefish" on pages 143 and 149 in *The Joy of Phonetics and Accents*, and play the pillow games to help open your voice and body to the possibility of speaking with this kind of "r."

An all-purpose IPA symbol for / r / in an accent

If you want to transcribe an r which is unlike any American-sounding "r" you have ever heard, you can use a small r which sits above the line / ʳ /· This is a catch-all symbol used with the understanding that it represents the type of "r" which is germane to the accent at hand. In a French accent it represents a uvular "r". It can also represent the "r" sound in a German accent, which like the French, is formed in the back of the mouth, though it may be breathier, and less trilled. In a British accent / ʳ / represents what is called a tap trill, which can occur in a word like "very" or, between words in a phrase like "there is." In a Scots accent, the symbol may appear several times in a row, to signify a longer trill, or burr.

Games in *The Joy of Phonetics and Accents*

The games in *The Joy of Phonetics and Accents* (on pages 43-46) were invented to give you facility with the IPA as well as to help you to deepen your relationship with each sound. The games can be used to explore texts, because they allow you to experience the sounds of a poem or monologue. Use these questions to stimulate your thinking and to record your discoveries.

Inventing Language, on page 43 of *The Joy of Phonetics and Accents*.

Draw the shapes of the symbols you recall from "Inventing Language."

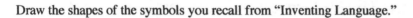

Which sounds provoked a strong response? Describe your response.

Diphthong Game, on page 43 of *The Joy of Phonetics and Accents*.

Draw the shapes of the symbols you recall from "Diphthong Game."

What, if any, images came to you during this exercise?

Passing Sound Around, on page 46 of *The Joy of Phonetics and Accents*

Draw the shapes of the symbols you recall from "Passing Sound Around."

Which of the sounds strike you as having a distinct personality?

Which sounds were most fun to play with?

Drawn to Sound, on page 44 of *The Joy of Phonetics and Accents*.

Which sounds called to you? Draw the shapes of the symbols you recall from "Drawn to Sound."

Which sound was your favorite?

What were you feeling during the exercise?

Symphony, on page 46 of *The Joy of Phonetics and Accents*.

Draw the shapes of the symbols you recall from the class exercise "Symphony."

Which of the sounds reminded you of musical instruments?

How would you describe your musical ensemble? Did your "symphony" resemble a band, orchestra, jazz band, acoustic ensemble or rock band?

The Soundalogue, on page 45 of *The Joy of Phonetics and Accents*.

What interested you most about your classmates' use of the "Soundalogue?" Did you hear any shifts in pronunciation from the way he/she usually speaks? Did he/she use voice differently?

How was your experience of your monologue different from usual? Were you aware of any shifts in the way you thought or felt? Were your images different?

Improv Game, on page 45 of *The Joy of Phonetics and Accents*.

What discoveries did you make while using sounds to communicate?

What observations did you make of other actors work during the game?

Finding your Monologue, on page 46 of *The Joy of Phonetics and Accents*.

What sounds seemed to carry the meaning of the monologue for you?

What sounds seemed to contain the character's feeling?

Were there any repeated sounds that gave you a clue as to the feelings or thoughts of the character?

What other discoveries did you make about the relationship of the sounds to character?

Articulation: Exploring the Energies of the Consonants

If your breath is free and your jaw is released; if the back of your tongue is relaxed and your soft palate limber, then the front of your tongue and your lips will be free for articulation. But, you may still need to stimulate the muscles of articulation to achieve the greater muscularity that is required for stage speaking and for many dialects.

Clear speaking rarely is accomplished merely by doing articulation exercises. It often requires quite a bit of work and time to release tension so that your voice is coming forward and arriving at your articulators. It is useful to take a voice class or study voice privately with a person who teaches voice production for actors. If you have tension in your throat, then working on articulation will not yield clarity. An actor's speech must be emotionally connected, appropriate to character, true to the text. Just as you would not impose your own habitual behaviors and tensions on a character, you would not impose your habitual habits and tensions on a character's speech. Your voice must be capable of power as well as subtlety. Your range of pitch, rhythms and dynamics must be great enough to serve the range in the text.

Clear speech is easy for you to speak and easy for others to hear. You are training to be a finely tuned athlete--your lips are receivers and releasers of vibration; your tongue is a gymnast; the gymnasium is the open cavity of your mouth. You train like a musician, dancer, or tennis player, working on individual muscles and integrating them with the whole. Do each part of the work with an awareness of your purpose--to communicate. Be conscious of your focus, your images and your changes in thinking and feeling as you play with sounds. Use sounds to communicate; don't just go through the motions. Let the words reflect your thought, even when some percentage of your mind is occupied with training your lips and tongue. The more specific your thought, the clearer your articulation.

In order for you to remain connected to thought, you must remain connected to your breath. Imagine that your incoming breath is the dropping in of the thought, and that the outgoing sounds of your voice are releasing your thought.

Workout One: Pleasurable Plosives

Stretch through your body, yawning. Stretch your legs, your arms. Slowly drop down through your spine and then uncurl back up through your spine, releasing your belly muscles. Sigh with relief on breath. Let your neck drop forward off your spine, releasing your head to gravity. Roll your neck to one side, so that your ear is close to your shoulder, letting gravity stretch your neck muscles. Let your jaw release. Roll your neck to the opposite side; let your jaw hang; let your tongue hang to gravity. Float your neck back up on top of your spine. Sigh with relief on vibrations, dropping down through your spine again. Let your torso hang to gravity while you blow through your lips, letting them flutter. Phonetically, a voiceless lip flutter is transcribed / ββββββ / and a voiced lip flutter is transcribed / *βββββ* /. Slowly uncurl back up through your spine, letting the muscles of your face hang to gravity, allowing your belly to be loose and your breath to be free.

As you stand, massage the skin of your face with your hands, allowing your bottom jaw to hang loosely. Massage your jaw muscles. Picture the bones at the hinge of your jaw and let your bottom jaw really hang. Sigh with relief several times, out past your jaw--first sigh breath, then sigh on the vibrations of your voice, *huuuuuh*.

Become aware of your tongue. Let your tongue relax on the floor of your mouth, adding weight to your jaw. Stretch your tongue all the way our of your mouth until you feel the back of your tongue stretch, then let it slide back in your mouth relaxed. Sigh with relief over your tongue, *huuuuuuuuuuuuuuuh*.

Yawn as your jaw drops easily, stretching your soft palate, opening the back of your throat. Then let your throat relax, your jaw and your tongue relax and blow vibrations onto your lips *ββββββββββββββ*.

94

Sigh a hum onto your lips and feel the vibrations arrive there easily. Stretch your lips wide using your fingers, then let them go and *ββββββββββββ* again. Yawn, feeling the back of your throat open. Sigh and *ββββββββββ* still feeling the openness in your throat. Sigh a hum onto your lips and see if the vibrations feel more free. See if you feel more vibrations.

Move your tongue around between your lips and your teeth, exploring the space between your lips and teeth. Stretch and relax your lips in several different ways: purse them and release; grimace and release; sneer and release; make fish lips and release; stretch them over your teeth and release; move them to the sides and release. Then flutter your lips again. Stretch your lips with your fingers.

Watch yourself in the mirror, so that you see your lips moving and your jaw hanging free. Let your lips come together and explode with "p." Explore the energy needed for "p;" what is the smallest amount of energy required? What is the most efficient "p?" Play with the most explosive "p," the most precise "p," the noisiest "p," the most angry "p," the most humorous "p." Play with the following words and see if you can sense what kind of "p" your lips choose for each.

pickle   plum   passion   pristine   pissed off   pocket   pray   lollipop   moppet   ripped   scrappy

Now practice releasing "p" into the neutral whispered "uh" with an awareness of what "p" can communicate:

puh puh puh puh puh puh puh puh

Add rhythm by distinguishing between strong and weak beats:

puh puh puh puh **puh** puh puh puh

Change the rhythm:
puh puh puh **puh** puh puh puh **puh**
puh puh **puh** puh puh puh **puh** puh
puh **puh** puh **puh** puh **puh** puh **puh**
puh puh puh **puh** puh puh **puh** puh puh

Answer these questions for yourself: Do you notice which parts of your lips want to come together for the "p?" The dry parts? The wet parts? Or the parts of your lips at the spot where the wet and dry meet? Which is most efficient in your use of energy? Which would allow you to articulate "p"s most quickly? Which is most pleasurable?
Flutter your lips: ƀƀƀƀƀƀƀƀƀƀƀƀƀ. Then add vibrations: ββββββββββββββββ. Let your lips come together and explode with a "b." What is the smallest amount of energy needed for "b?" Find the most bombastic "b," the most bubbly "b," the most baby-size "b," the most boisterous "b." Play with the following words and feel what kind of energy your lips want to bring to the "b."

brisk   blot   blink   brass   imbibe   baggy   elbow   forbid   flabby   scab   fabulous   believe

Now practice releasing the voiced "b" into the voiced "uh" with an awareness of what "b" can communicate:

buh buh buh buh buh buh buh buh buh

Add rhythm:
buh buh buh **buh** buh buh **buh** buh buh
buh buh **buh** buh buh **buh** buh buh **buh**
buh buh buh buh **buh** buh buh buh

Watching yourself in the mirror, allow your jaw to release again. Let your tongue slide out onto your bottom lip so that the tip is even with your bottom lip. Let it relax there on your lip. Now let the tip of your tongue bend upwards so that it touches your upper lip. Then let your tongue release back onto your bottom lip. Up--release. Up--release; leaving your jaw relaxed and the back of your tongue relaxed. Remember, your tongue is a gymnast. Now let your tongue relax back into your mouth, the tip of your tongue right behind your bottom front teeth. Repeat the gymnastic activity of up-release, but this time let your tongue touch your gum ridge--just behind your top teeth, then release back down. Each time, your tongue relaxes down.

Flutter your tongue onto your top lip. Flutter your tongue onto your gum ridge. Add vibrations. You're trilling!

Now touch your tongue to your gum ridge and let breath explode from behind your tongue, "t." Leave your jaw relaxed so that your tongue reaches for your gum ridge without the "help" of your jaw. Explore the sound--find the most efficient "t," the messiest "t," the most effortful "t," the most pleasurable "t." Speak the following words with an awareness of the different feelings of "t" in each word:

tickle   trickle   taste   twirl   nasty   little   rattling   flat   splat   platitude   fraternize   trust

Do you whisper the "t" in each word, or are some of the "t" sounds slightly voiced? Are some of them more explosive than others? Are some more precise than others?

Let the whispered "t" become the voiced "d." Look in the mirror to see if your jaw is still released as you release the "d." Alternate between the "t" and "d" being aware of the physical sensation of the sounds. See if you can let your tongue perform the same physical action for both sounds, so that the only difference between them is that "t" is whispered and "d" is voiced. Speak the following words with an awareness of the "d" in each word:

daft   drink   delicate   dead   distant   drunk   dawdle   old   proud   padding   pudding   skid

As you release the "t" and "d" into the neutral vowel, be aware of the openness in your throat and your mouth:

tuh tuh tuh tuuuuuuuuh   tuh tuh tuh tuuuuuuuuh
tuh tuh tuh tuuh tuuh tuuh   tuh tuh tuh tuuh tuuh tuuh
tuuh tuh tuh tuh tuh   tuuh tuh tuh tuh tuh

duh-duh duuuh duuuh duuuh   duh-duh duuuh duuuh duuuh
duh duh duh duh **duh** duh duh duh
duh **duh** duh **duh** duh **duh** duh **duh**

The blade of your tongue should feel like it's been used, engaged. It is **working**. The back of your tongue should be relaxed and your throat easily open. Relax your jaw again. Stretch and release throughout your entire body in order to eliminate any unwanted tension. Send your attention to the inside of your mouth. With the tip of your tongue behind your bottom teeth, stretch the middle of your tongue out; then relax your tongue back into your mouth. Sigh with relief and flutter your lips. Yawn and stretch through your body.

Yawn again and feel your soft palate stretch. Let your soft palate relax onto your tongue. Then yawn again and feel your soft palate stretch and then relax. Now let the middle of your tongue and your soft palate come together and explode in a whispered "k." Explore several places on your tongue and your hard and soft palates, to explode several differently-placed "k"s. Probably the most efficient "k" for most people occurs at the place where the soft palate and the hard palate meet, in the middle of the mouth. Find your most quiet "k." Your most scratchy "k;" the most sickly "k;" the most pristine "k;" the most pompous "k." Speak the following "k" words (some spelled with "c"):

kiss   crack   class   cause   picked   smacked   rank   brickle   prickly   lackey   key   calm

Release your jaw and feel the back of your throat opening up to release the neutral vowel in the following:

kuh kuh kuh kuh **kuh** kuh kuh kuh
kuh kuh kuh kuh **kuh** kuh kuh kuh

puh kuh puh kuh   **puh** kuh puh kuh
tuh kuh tuh kuh   **tuh** kuh tuh kuh

Can you flutter your soft palate and tongue together? Another kind of trill!

Let the whispered "k" become the voiced "g." Look in the mirror to see if your jaw is still released as you release the "g." Alternate between the "k" and "g" being aware of the physical sensation of the sounds. See if you can let your tongue and soft palate perform the same physical action for both sounds, so that the only difference between them is that "k" is whispered and "g" is voiced. Speak the following words with an awareness of the "g" in each word:

giggle   gaggle   snag   pig   gout   grease   fragment   plagued   sniggled   vogue   glean   glass

Now go to rhythms, with an awareness of your throat opening for the vowel:

guh guh guh **guh** guh guh **guh** guh guh **guh** guh guh
guh-guh guuuh guuuh guuuh   guh-guh guuuh guuuh guuuh

Now add pitch. Use a five-tone major scale:

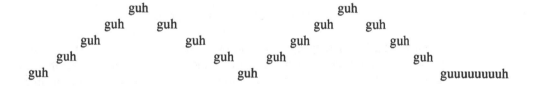

Work for ease and flexibility as you speak the following:

Rubber baby buggy bumpers.

Visualize the image of those bumpers. Does it change the way your articulators respond?
Tell someone else about those bumpers. Does having a listener change the way your articulators respond?
Sing it to them. Does that change anything?

Use the following "tongue twisters" to engage your articulators and enhance your awareness. Use them to communicate **while** exercising your articulators.

Billy Burton buttoned his bright brown boots and blue coat before breakfast began.
Dashing Daniel defied David to deliver Dora from the dawning danger.

Gertrude Gray gazed at the grey goose gaily.

Big blue blisters bleeding badly.

The green grub goes to the green grass.

Dimpled Dinah danced in dainty dimity down the dunes.

Tiny Tim toddles to the tiny toddlers' toyshop.

Is there any pleasant peasant present?

The conundrum constructed by the communist was catastrophical.

What a to-do to die today at a quarter of two to two
Is a thing distinctly hard to say and harder still to do.

Peter Piper picked a peck of pickled peppers
A peck of pickled peppers did Peter Piper pick.
If Peter Piper picked a peck of pickled peppers,
Where's the peck of pickled peppers Peter Piper picked?

Workout Two: Passionate Fricatives

Feel the friction in your mouth as you speak the following:

mesmerize   zither   razor   wizard   ozone   please   zoo   zebras   frizzy   busy   prize

Speak *"zzzzzzzzz"* as you move the smallest bit of your tongue tip up and down behind your teeth. Move your tongue tip slowly to discover where the most vibration occurs--where you feel the most "buzz." Can you feel the tip of your tongue actually vibrate? If your tongue tip is just behind your teeth--upper or lower teeth--you will be able to enjoy a clear, firm "z."

Experiment with the air pressure behind your teeth until you feel the most vibration--does more pressure yield more or less vibration?

Find the range of pitches possible for your "z." Can you buzz up and down 2 octaves on "z?" Which pitches are easiest to produce--the lowest ones or the highest ones?

Eliminate all of the "hiss" from your "z" so it is pure vibration. Sing the tune of "Frere Jacques" on "zzzzz."

```
                                                    z                  z
                        ZZZZZZ     ZZZZZZ  ZZ  ZZ          ZZ  ZZ
                           ZZZ        ZZZ          ZZ             ZZ
        ZZZ        ZZZ  ZZZ        ZZZ                 ZZZ           ZZZ
   ZZZ        ZZZ
ZZZ        ZZZZZZ     ZZZ                              ZZZ        ZZZ  ZZZ   ZZZZZZZZZZ    ZZZZZZ
                                                                  ZZZ           ZZZ
```

Sing your most vibratory "z" and then suddenly eliminate all vibrations, allowing a small amount of breath to flow between your teeth. Imagine the new sound as razor sharp. Then, begin with "ssssss....," slowly add vibration until the whisper is gone and only the buzzing "zzzzz" remains. Alternate "ssszzzssszzzsssssssszzzzzzz."

Finish all of the following words with a firm, clear, relaxed sound of "z."

ceilings   floors   walls   beds   tables   chairs   goes   comes   runs   crashes   prances   flies   falls

Speak the following phrases :

backs, fronts and sides   bats and balls   pots and pans   cups and glasses   seconds, minutes, hours and days

Is there a pattern here?

Explore the vibrations of "v" between your top teeth and bottom lip. Vary the air pressure. Experiment with the placement of your lip beneath your teeth until you feel the most vibration. Find the most effortless, yet vibratory "vvvvv."

Slowly sing "vvvvv" from your lowest possible pitch to your highest clear vibration of "vvv." Then find your most pleasurable range of pitches. Then find your most thrilling range of pitches.

Play with the sound on your lower lip. Do different words inspire different experiences of "v"? Lengthen the "v" in each word and taste its full value.

suave   vicious   savory   viper   lavish   cave   favorite   sieve   wave   villainous   very

Let yourself travel on a continuum between "vvvvvvv..............fffffff" taking vibrations away slowly until only breath remains between your bottom lip and top teeth. Then travel back from "fffffff" to "vvvvvvv" adding vibration until you have pure vibration.

Speak the following words feeling your articulators in the same positions for "v" and "f" but keeping each sound pure.

save--safe   vast--fast   vile--file   vender--fender   savor--safer   veer--fear   vie--fie

Let "vvvv" run down your spine and "zzzzzz" run back up your spine. Move these sounds through your body.
Let "fffff" travel over the surface of your skin and "ssssss" blow through your hair.
Use the following "tongue twisters" to practice your fricatives with ease and clarity.

Sally Sloop saw six sad sheep standing on the sea shore shamelessly shamming sleep.

Flora's fan fluttered feebly and her fine fingers fidgeted.

Sister Suzy sneezes slightly, slicing succulent shallots.

Virile Victor vanquished vain vendors.

Voluptuous Velma visited invincible Vincent.

Vain Valerie invited Vinnie's advances.

Felonious Freddie fired five feckless farts.

Featherbrained Phillip frightened fly-fishers' floating flotilla.

Flowery Phoebe flounced finally, affecting frantic frailty.

Sound and Meaning

Are meanings "encoded" in the vowels and diphthongs of a text? The playwright or poet writes with an awareness of the sounds of language, whether making choices consciously, semi-unconsciously or even unconciously. Your conscious exploration of a text may reveal a new layer of meaning and experience for you. You may find that particular vowel sounds evoke feeling for you, much as you might find an emotional connection to a particular color. Choose a color and underline the long vowels and the diphthongs in "End of Summer" by Stanley Kunitz. Speak the text, allowing the length of the long vowels to inform your speaking. Elongate the long vowels just a bit more than you would usually do. Speak the text of the first stanza of Alfred Lord Tennyson's "Sweet and Low." Write the IPA symbols for the long vowels and diphthongs above the words. How does your attention to long vowels inform the rhythm of your speaking? How does the rhythm affect the feeling conveyed in your voice?

Sweet and Low, by Alfred Lord Tennyson

Sweet and low, sweet and low,

Wind of the western sea,

Low, low, breathe and blow,

Wind of the western sea!

Over the rolling waters go,

Come from the dying moon, and blow,

Blow him again to me;

While my little one, while my pretty one, sleeps.

Sound Symbolism

While single, isolated sounds do not always elicit meaning, a playful exploration of individual sounds paves the way to an aesthetic understanding of language. This in turn, awakens a command of language, and heightens appreciation of literature.

Words such as "hum," "zip," "buzz," "chirp," "squeak," "purr," and "twitter" not only suggest action, but also reproduce the sounds of natural events. Meanings can be deduced from the sounds of these words; this is somewhat out of keeping with the linguistic principle that "sounds in and of themselves do not carry meaning." However, David Crystal in *The Cambridge Encyclopedia of Language* states that "There are an interesting number of exceptions to the general rule--cases where native speakers feel that there is some kind of meaningful connection between a sound, or cluster of sounds, and properties of the outside world. This phenomenon is known as sound symbolism, also called phonaesthesia (when focusing on the aesthetic values of sounds) or onomatopoeia (when focusing on the use of sound in poetry.)"

Observing that words sometimes copy the noises of the things they represent--onomotopocia--Crystal brings our attention to "bang, clip-clop, cough, cuckoo, knock, murmur, rat-a-tat, whoosh, yackety-yak and zoom." Speaking to the subjective nature of sound symbolism he adds, "Sometimes we can do no more than express a vague feeling that the word is somehow appropriate to a thing, without being able to say why."

In addition to words which echo natural sounds--onomotopoeia--philologists have theorized that words carry meaning through mimetic gestures of the lips and tongue. To quote Richard Paget: "What drove man to the invention of speech was, as I imagine, not so much the need for expressing his thoughts, (for that might have been done quite satisfactorily by bodily gesture) as the difficulty of "talking with his hands full." It was the continual use of man's hands for craftsmanship, the chase, and the beginnings of art and agriculture, that drove him to find other methods of expressing his ideas--namely by a specialized [audible] pantomime of the tongue and lips."

In his book *The Language of Gesture*, Macdonald Critchley surveyed the research of philologists in the field of sound symbolism. He writes that "an intimate alliance between the sound of a word and its meaning can be traced in about four fifths of short words in the English language;" and that the same principles apply to other languages. He goes on: "In English the vowel sound *ahh* refers to anything which is wide open, large, spacious or flat; " (e.g. lot, farm, car)
i and *ee* refer to that which is high, forward placed, or little (e.g. *steeple, teeny, peak, tiny;*)
aw connotes a cavity (e.g. *yawn*)
and *oo* something enclosed, full, tubular, or elongated (e.g. *room, tube, loop.*)
In the same way specific meanings are linked with various consonants. For instance, *s* and *z* suggest something reaching forwards or upwards (e.g. *send, steep, gaze, stare*)
l indicates motion to or from a point (e.g. *length, long, leave*)
and *sn* anything pertaining to the nose (*snort, snout, snuff, sneeze,* etc.) ...

The combination *fl* is said to suggest movement; usually up or inward (*fly, flow, flop*)
c r surrounding, containing, gripping, punching or bending (*crumble, crush, crack, cram*)
sl sliding back or down (*slide, slip, slither, slump, slim, slight, slow, slur*)
ump projecting, or inflated, or round (*hump, bump, dump, rump, lump, trump*)
m or *mb* enclosed (*room, tomb*)
sh a high, thin surface or layer (*shoot, shimmer, shore, shift, shirt, sheet, shin*)
st drawn up, hold up, or contract (*stand, still, stop, start, stem*)
str extending from here to there (*stretch, street, strand, stream.*) "

Phonetic Pillow Game For Exploring Sound Symbolism

Phonetic pillow games can be played with gesture-based words, such as crunch, pop, zip, snap, clap, giggle, tap. In these games, the pillow which represents the most gestural feature of a word, such as the "t" in "tap," is passed from player to player as each says the word. The style in which they say the word will be evocative of the action of tapping--percussive, staccato, etc. Each player should be encouraged to repeat the movement and sound of the word several times before passing the phonetic pillow on to another player.

The following gestural interpretations were set down by linguists Macdonald Critchley, Richard Paget and Otto Jepperson. They will be useful in helping you pick words with symbolic sounds and mouth gestures. Use these words to play the Phonetic Pillow sound symbolism game. Toss the appropriate vowel pillow for each word below in a gesturally evocative way:

Small Gestures may accompany words like:
> *bee, seed, teeny, beep, sneak, key, pea, bean, bit, tip, sip, pill, little, bib, kiss, wrists*

Gestures made high in the air:
> *tree, bee, leaf, leap*

Close gestures:
> *cheek, ear, near, knee*

Large gestures:
> *wall, tall, call, fall*

Open, expansive gestures:
> *lawn, dawn*

Long, hollow, forward pointing gestures:
> *loop, hoop, moon*

Hollow gestures:
> *tube, room, pool, boot, womb, flute, toot, loop, hoop*

Forward pointing gestures:
> *tool, shoot, flute, root*

Large space gestures:
> *barn, far, star, large, arch, yard*

Flat gestures:
> *palm, calm*

Mouth Gestures

Because we use our lips when we speak, it could be said that our lips are "gesturing." Speak the words of Titania's monologue, below, and exaggerate your lips as gesture-makers. Then speak the text again, allowing your lip experience to inform your communication.

These are the forgeries of jealousy:
And never, since the middle summer's spring,
Met we on hill, in dale, forest, or mead,
By paved mountain or by rushy brook,
Or in the beached margent of the sea,
To dance our ringlets to the whistling wind,
But with thy brawls thou hast disturbed our sport.
Therefore the winds, piping to us in vain,
As in revenge, have sucked up from the sea
Contagious fogs; which, falling in the land,
Hath every pelting river made so proud,
That they have overborne their continents.
The ox hath therefore stretched his yoke in vain,
The plowman lost his sweat, and the green corn
Hath rotted ere his youth attained a beard;
The fold stands empty in the drowned field,
And crows are fatted with the murrion flock,
The nine men's morris is filed up with mud;
And the quaint mazes in the wanton green,
For lack of tread, are undistinguishable.
The human mortals want their winter here;
No night is now with hymn or carol blest.
Therefore the moon, the governess of the floods,
Pale in her anger, washes all the air,
That rheumatic diseases do abound.
And thorough this distemperature wen see
The seasons alter; hoary-headed frosts
Fall in the fresh lap of the crimson rose,
And on old Heim's thin and icy crown
An odorous chaplet of sweet summer buds
Is, in mockery, set. The spring, the summer,
The childing autumn, angry winter, change
Their wonted liveries; and the mazed world,
By their increase, now knows not which is which.
And this same progeny of evils comes
From our debate, from our dissension;
We are their parents and original.

Midsummer Night's Dream, II i

Did any of the words come more alive for you? Did your images change or become more vivid? How did lip awareness affect your speaking?

Use your lip awareness in speaking the following Sonnet. Let your lips round for / w / and for the vowels / ɔ /, / u /, / ʊ /, and diphthongs / oʊ /, / ɔr /, / aʊ /, / ʊr /. Feel the vibrations arrive on your lips for / m /, / v /, and / b /.

As a decrepit father takes delight
To see his active child do deeds of youth,
So I, made lame by Fortune's dearest spite,
Take all my comfort of thy worth and truth.
For whether beauty, birth, or wealth, or wit,
Or any of these all, or all, or more,
Entitled in their parts do crowned sit,
I make my love engrafted to this store.
So then I am not lame, poor, nor despised
Whilst that this shadow doth such substance give
That I in thy abundance am sufficed
And by a part of all thy glory live.
　Look what is best, that best I wish in thee.
　This wish I have, then ten times happy me.

Does your attention to your lips affect the way you speak? Do your listeners get any additional meaning? Any more specific images?

Speak "All Day I Hear the Noise of Waters," by James Joyce. Let the long vowels and diphthongs have their length. Explore the rounding of your lips for the / oʊ /, / ɔr / and / w /.

All Day I Hear the Noise of Waters by James Joyce

All day I hear the noise of waters
　　Making moan,
Sad as the sea-bird is, when going
　　Forth alone,
He hears the winds cry to the waters'
　　Monotone.

The grey winds, the cold winds are blowing
　　Where I go.
I hear the noise of many waters
　　Far below.
All day, all night, I hear them flowing
　　To and fro.

Now, speak "Jabberwocky" by Lewis Carroll. Fully invest your body and your voice in each word. See if the words tell you what they mean.

Jabberwocky, Lewis Carroll

'Twas brillig, and the slithy toves
Did gyre and gimble in the wabe;
All mimsy were the borogoves,
And the momeraths outgrabe.

Beware the Jabberwock, my son!
The jaws that bite, the claws that catch!
Beware the Jubjub bird, and shun
The frumious Bandersnatch!

He took his vorpal sword in hand;
Long time the manxome foe he sought
So rested he by the Tumtum tree,
And stood awhile in thought.

And, as in uffish thought he stood,
The Jabberwock, with eyes of flame,
Came whiffling through the tulgey wood,
And burbled as it came!

One, two! One, two! And through and through
The vorpal blade went snicker-snack!
He left it dead, and with its head
He went galumphing back.

"And hast thou slain the Jabberwock?
Come to my arm, my beamish boy!
O frabjous day! Callooh! Callay!"
He chortled in his joy.

Ask another person, a classmate or the whole group, to tell you what images they got from you as you spoke the text. What meaning came through on "vorpal," for example? What action was "galumphing?" What does "beamish" describe? Do others get a general feeling from you? Or a specific image?

Playing the Consonants

The American Heritage Dictionary, has an astounding twenty-six different definitions of the verb "to play." The authors have cited several of them below.

To occupy oneself in amusement, sport, or other recreation; To take part in a game; To act in jest or sport; To behave or converse in a sportive or playful way; To act, especially in a dramatic production; To perform on an instrument; To emit sound or be sounded in performance; To be received or accepted; To move or seem to move quickly, lightly, or irregularly; To perform or act (a role or part) in a dramatic performance; To pretend to be; mimic the activities of; To use or manipulate, especially for one's own interests.

Which of these definitions might suit the journeys you have been undertaking with the vowel and consonant sounds for the pursuit of discovery, pleasure, self-awareness, reconditioning and awakening your senses?

Which of the definitions sparks your interest or suggests a new way of working with sounds?

Use Gerard Manley Hopkins' "The Windhover" to explore "playing" with **consonants**. First speak the words aloud, to discover what the words do to you. Next, slightly elongate or "play" the / m /, / n / and / ŋ / in the text, aware of the effect on the rhythm. Feel the vibrations of the nasal sounds / m /, / n / and / ŋ / lightly in your mouth; feel the vibrations travel through your body. Remember the definition of the word "play": "to use or manipulate, especially for ones own interests?"

What other consonant sounds predominate? Let the / s / gently flow through your teeth and snake through your body each time you come upon it in the text. Let the plosive / b / burst forth from your lips. Feel the wind of the / f / as it passes over your bottom lip.

The Windhover, by Gerard Manley Hopkins

I caught this morning morning's minion, king-
    dom of daylight's dauphin, dapple-dawn-drawn Falcon,
      in his riding
    Of the rolling level underneath him steady air, and
      striding
High there, how he rung upon the rein of a wimpling wing
In his ecstasy! then off, off forth on swing.
    As a skate's heel sweeps smooth on a bow-bend; the
      hurl and gliding
    Rebuffed the big wind. My heart in hiding
Stirred for a bird,--the achieve of, the mastery of the thing!

Brute beauty and valor and act, oh, air, pride, plume, here
    Buckle! AND the fire that breaks from thee then, a billion
Times told lovelier, more dangerous, O my chevalier!

    No wonder of it; sheer plod makes plow down sillion
Shine, and blue-bleak embers, ah my dear,
    Fall, gall themselves, and gash gold-vermillion.

The natural rhythms of the language in Hopkin's "The Leaden Echo and the Golden Echo," below, might suggest that you could be using the definition of the word "play" in your exploration: "To move or seem to move quickly, lightly, or irregularly." Spend time with this piece, speaking it aloud several times. Let your whole body respond to its irregular rhythms. Speak it around the group, each person taking one line, playing each consonant as it arrives on your lips, your tongue, your soft palate. Feel the length of the continuant consonants--the music of the vibrations. Allow the singable consonants to have pitch. Feel the explosive quality of the plosive consonants. Play the friction of the fricatives. Use the definition of the word "play": "to behave or converse in a sportive or playful way."

The Leaden Echo and the Golden Echo, Gerard Manley Hopkins

The Leaden Echo

How to keep--is there any any, is there none such, nowhere
    known some, bow or brooch or braid or brace, lace, latch
      or catch or key to keep
Back beauty, keep it, beauty, beauty, beauty,...from vanishing away?
O is there no frowning of these wrinkles, ranked wrinkles deep,
Down? no waving off of these most mournful messengers,
    still messengers, sad and stealing messengers of grey?
No there's none, there's none, O no there's none,
Nor can you long be, what you now are, called fair,
Do what you may do, what, do what you may,
And wisdom is early to despair:
Be beginning; since, no, nothing can be done
To keep at bay
Age and age's evils, hoar hair,
Ruck and wrinkle, dropping, dying, death's worst, winding
    sheets, tombs and worms and tumbling to decay;
So be beginning to despair, to despair,
Despair, despair, despair, despair.

The Golden Echo
        Spare!
There is one, yes I have one (Hush there!);
Only not within seeing of the sun,
Not within the singeing of the strong sun,
Tall sun's tingeing, or treacherous the tainting of the earth's air,
Somewhere elsewhere there is ah well where! one,
One. Yes I can tell such a key, I do know such a place,
Where whatever's prized and passes of us, everything that's
        fresh and fast flying of us, seems to us sweet of us and
        swiftly away with, done away with, undone,
Undone, done with, soon done with, and yet dearly and dangerously sweet
Of us, the wimpled-water-dimpled, not-by-morning-matched face,
The flower of beauty, fleece of beauty, too too apt to, ah! to fleet,
Never fleets more, fastened with the tenderest truth
To its own best being and its loveliness of youth; it is an ever
        lastingness of, O it is an all youth!
Come then your ways and airs and looks, locks, maiden hear,
        gallantry and gaiety and grace,
Winning ways, airs innocent, maiden manners, sweet looks,
        loose locks, long locks, lovelocks, gaygear, going gallant, girlgrace-----
Resign them, sign them seal them, send them, motion them with breath,
And with sights souring, soaring sighs deliver
Them; beauty-in-the-ghost, deliver it, early now, long before death
Give beauty back, beauty, beauty, beauty back to God,
        Beauty's self and beauty's giver.

"Playing the Consonants" is a concept coined by Arthur Lessac, in his book *The Use and Training of the Human Voice*. Lessac likens each consonant to a musical instrument or sound effect. Read aloud "Kubla Khan" by Samuel Taylor Coleridge. Play each consonant as if it were a different musical instrument--a clarinet; an oboe; a violin; a viola; a cello; a French horn; a snare drum; a tympani; a flute. Rather than assigning a musical instrument to each, see if the consonants can choose their own instruments.

Kubla Khan by Samuel Taylor Coleridge

In Xanadu did Kubla Khan
    A stately pleasure-dome decree:
Where Alph, the sacred river, ran
Through caverns measureless to man
    Down to a sunless sea.
So twice five miles of fertile ground
With walls and towers were girdled round:
And here were gardens bright with sinuous rills,
Where blossomed many an incense-bearing tree,
And here were forests ancient as the hills,
Enfolding sunny spots of greenery.

But oh? that deep romantic chasm which slanted
Down the green hill athwart a cedarn cover!
A savage place! as holy and enchanted
As e're beneath a waning moon was haunted
by woman wailing for her demon-lover!
And from this chasm, with ceaseless turmoil seething,
As if this earth in fast thick pants were breathing,
A mighty fountain momently was forced,
Amid whose swift half-intermitted burst
Huge fragments vaulted like rebounding hail,
Or chaffy grain beneath the thresher's flail;
And 'mid these dancing rocks at once and ever
It flung up momently the sacred river.
Five miles meandering with a mazy motion
Through wood and dale the sacred river ran,
Then reached the caverns measureless to man,
And sank in tumult to a lifeless ocean:
And 'mid this tumult Kubla heard from far
Ancestral voices prophesying war!

The shadow of the dome of pleasure
    Floated midway on the waves;
    Where was heard the mingled measure
    From the fountain and the caves.

It was a miracle of rare device,
A sunny pleasure-dome with caves of ice!
   A damsel with a dulcimer
   In a vision once I saw;
   It was an Abyssinian maid,
   And on her dulcimer she played,
   Singing of Mount Abora.

   Could I revive within me
   Her symphony and song,
   To such a deep delight 'twould win me,
That with music loud and long,
I would build that dome in air,
That sunny dome? those caves of ice!
And all should cry, Beware! Beware!
His flashing eyes, his floating hair!
Weave a circle round him thrice,
And close your eyes with holy dread,
For he on honey-dew hath fed,
And drunk the milk of Paradise.

Which consonants chose which instruments?

Grouping Sounds by their "Personalities"

In this section you will put sounds in groups in order to make generalizations about them; you can then assign various characteristics to them based on the groups in which they have been placed. English sounds can be categorized as vowels, consonants or diphthongs. These groupings are extremely useful; they allow you to talk about the characteristics common to all "personalities" in a group. For example, all vowels are open sounds; all diphthongs are composed of two vowel sounds; all consonants involve closure or partial closure of articulators. On the other hand, grouping can be limiting. When sounds are identified primarily with academic labels, i.e. fricatives, bilabials, etc. exploration can grind to a halt. Such labels promote an arid, theoretical analysis of sounds, devoid of visceral connection. Exploration requires an atmosphere of openness and acceptance of the new; the embodiment of the unusual. Remember, each sound has its own unique personality. Use the groupings to add to your experience of the sounds.

Vowel Sounds can be grouped by:
---how the space in the mouth is shaped by the position of the tongue
---the extent to which lips are rounded, spread or relaxed
---length or duration of the sound
---resonant quality and intrinsic pitch of the sound (see vowel ladder on page 43 of this workbook)
---the area of your body in which they seem to "live" (see resonating scale on page 43 of this workbook)

Consonants can be grouped by:
---articulators involved (two-lips, teeth and lips, etc.)
---the way in which the sound is released (plosives, affricates, etc.)
---presence or lack of vibration in the sound (voiced or unvoiced)
---relative duration of the sound (continuant or non-continuant)

You could group sounds many other ways. What about sounds used in a particular region:
----Sounds used in the Scottish Highlands accent
----Nasal vowels, as used in a French Accent
----Sounds used in African accents that are not used in English, such as clicks and other ingressive sounds (sounds made on an incoming breath)
----The first sounds a baby makes
----The sounds you find most soothing
----Sounds that mimic animal noises
----Sounds you find annoying
----Sounds you personally connect with anger, joy, sadness
----Sounds you don't commonly use in your own speech

Draw the phonetic symbols for sounds which are made by the action of your two lips touching. In some sounds they will touch and spring apart. In other sounds, the lips will vibrate together loosely.

Draw the phonetic symbol for each sound which maintains a large mouth opening with the jaw dropped.

Draw the phonetic symbol for each vowel sound which is very short in length.

Draw the phonetic symbol for each consonant sound which can be of long duration.

Draw the phonetic symbol for consonants which include the teeth as articulators.

Draw the phonetic symbol for the sounds you like to taste.

Invent your own sound-personality group:_____
Draw the symbols in that group.

Invent another sound-personality group:_____
Draw the symbols in that group.

Divide the following symbols into three groups: vowels, consonants and diphthongs.

i ɪ ɛ æ a ɑ ə ʌ ɚ ɝ ɒ ɔ o ʊ u aɪ ɔɪ aʊ

oʊ eɪ o e ju b p g k d t v f h ð j l m n r s

ʃ w ʤ θ z ʒ ŋ ʧ hw

VOWELS

CONSONANTS

DIPHTHONGS

Divide the following consonants into two categories: voiced consonants and unvoiced consonants. Voiced consonants are sounded, they have vibration. Unvoiced consonants are whispered; they involve articulators and breath only.

b p g k d t v f h ð j l m n r s ʃ w ʤ ʧ z ʒ ŋ θ hw

VOICED

UNVOICED

Divide the following consonants into cognate pairs. Consonant cognates are voiced and voiceless counterparts formed in the same way. For example / t / and / d / are consonant cognates:

b p k g θ d t v f s ʃ ʤ ʧ z ʒ

Draw the consonants which belong to each of the following categories.

TWO LIPS (labial)_____ _____ _____

SOFT PALATE (velar)_____ _____ _____

LABIAL-DENTAL (Top front teeth and bottom lip)_____ _____

ALVEOLAR RIDGE (Gum ridge behind top teeth)_____ _____ _____ _____

Consonants are often put in descriptive groups based on the way they release from your mouth. Plosives are made with an "explosion" between two surfaces. Draw the Plosives.

PLOSIVES_____ _____ _____ _____ _____ _____

Fricatives are made with "friction" between two surfaces. Draw the fricatives.

FRICATIVES_____ _____ _____ _____ _____ _____ _____ _____ _____ _____

Affricates are made of a fricative and a plosive combined. Draw the affricates.

AFFRICATES_____ _____

Nasals are made with the mouth passage closed; the vibration is sent through the nose. Draw the nasal consonants.

NASALS_____ _____ _____

Liquids sometimes have the quality of a vowel. Draw them.

LIQUIDS_____ _____

114

Sounds into Words

You have explored the sounds of language by speaking them fully, allowing them access to your body and your feelings and your memories. If you have been playing with the IPA pillows as well, you have "touched" the sounds with all parts of your body, hugged them and thrown them across the room. Sounds are now encoded in your experience. Each time you re-experience one of these sounds, you will have unconscious access to everything you have stirred up. If each sound carries a separate experience, a whole word could tap four or five experiences, one after another. If you truly commit to speaking all sounds in all words, a sentence could communicate a world of experience, emotion, image. This level of communication is a different one from the *meaning* of the word. Sound wedded with image delivers much more than mere intellectual meaning.

Reading IPA: Sounding Out Words

Reading IPA is a skill that allows you to "hear" precise pronunciations of words in a given accent. You may use it to remind yourself of certain pronunciations you have chosen; for instance, if you encounter an unfamiliar word and don't want to forget how to say it, if you want to keep yourself consistent in your own pronunciation of a word, or if you want to assist yourself in learning to speak accents. Often all you'll need is a little reminder in your script--a single IPA symbol reminding you that the pronunciation you're using for "doth" is / ʌ / rather than / ɒ /. At other times, you may want to write some of your text in IPA in order to become aware of patterns of sound--repetition, rhyme, alliteration, assonance, etc. Your voice/speech director may use written IPA to communicate the accent which will be used in a production and as a shorthand to communicate notes to actors. You'll need to be able to read the IPA quickly. Because you've also used the IPA as an exploration, the symbols will carry your experience with them.

In order to sound out written IPA, you need to be able to "hear" the component parts of words. Words can have as many as five or even more syllables and syllables aren't indicated in IPA (although accent marks are sometimes used in IPA.) *Longman's Pronunciation Dictionary* by J.C. Wells defines syllables as follows:

> In phonetics, a **syllable** is a group of sounds that are pronounced together. Every English word consists of one or more complete syllables.
> **glad** consists of one syllable: **'glæd**
> **coming** consists of two syllables: **'kʌm and ɪŋ**
> so does **valley: 'væl** and **i**
> **tobacco** consists of three syllables: **tə 'bæk,** and **əʊ or oʊ**
> Each syllable contains one vowel, and only one. This vowel may be preceded or followd by one or more consonants. The vowel itself may be a short vowel, a long vowel, or a diphthong; or, if it is the weak vowel ə, it may be combined with a nasal or liquid to give a syllabic consonant. All four types appear in the example
> **lubrication luː b rɪ 'keɪ ʃᵊn**

Read this transcription of a passage from Gilbert and Sullivan's *Iolanthe*. Note the multisyllabic words.

/lʌv ʌnrɪkwaɪtɪd rɑbz mi əv maɪ rɛst

lʌv hoʊpləs lʌv maɪ ɑrdnt soʊl ɪnkʌmbɚz

lʌv naɪtmɛrlaɪk laɪz hɛvi ɑn maɪ tʃɛst

ænd wivz ɪtsɛlf ɪntʊ maɪ mɪdnaɪt slʌmbɚz

wɛn jʊr laɪɪŋ əweɪk wɪð ə dɪzml hɛdeɪk

ænd rɪpoʊz ɪz tæbud baɪ æŋzaɪti

aɪ kənsid ju meɪ juz ɛnɪ læŋgwɪʤ ju tʃuz

tʊ ɪndʌlʤ ɪn wɪðaʊt ɪmpropraɪti/

115

How many syllables are in each of the following words?

ɪmproprаɪti _____   rɪpoʊz_____   ʌnrɪkwaɪtɪd _____

ɪndʌlʤ_____   naɪtmɛrlaɪk _____

Stress is a feature of syllables. According to *Longman's Dictionary*:

> A stressed syllable is one that carries a rhythmic beat. It is marked by greater loudness than unstressed syllables, and often by pitch-prominence or greater duration, or more clearly defined vowel qualities.

> An accent is the placement of intonational pitch-prominence (=higher or lower pitch than the surroundings) on a word. Speakers choose to accent certain words (or to de-accent others) because of the particular meanings they wish to convey in a particular situation. Accents can fall on stressed syllables. Thus to accent the word **collapse** kə 'læps the pitch-prominence goes on the syllable læps, but in **tumble** 'tʌm bᵊl on the syllable tʌm.

Here is a transcription of another piece of "The Nightmare Song" from *Iolanthe*:

/fɔr jʊr breɪn ɪz ɑn faɪr
ðə bɛdkloʊz kənspaɪr əv juzʊəl slʌmbɚ tʊ plʌndɚ ju
fɝst jʊr kaʊntɚpeɪn goʊz
ænd ʌnkʌvɚz jʊr toʊz
ænd jʊr ʃit slɪps dɪmjʊrli frəm ʌndɚ ju
ðɛn ðə blæŋkɪtɪŋ tɪklz
ju fil laɪk mɪkst pɪklz
soʊ tɛrɪbli ʃɑrp ɪz ðə prɪkɪŋ
ænd jʊr hɑt ænd jʊr krɔs
ænd ju tʌmbl ænd tɔs
tɪl ðɛrz nʌθɪŋ twɪkst ju ænd ðə tɪkɪŋ/

From the preceding passage, pick out the words with more than one syllable. Divide them into syllables in phonetics below and indicate the primary stress with a stress mark before the accented syllable.

_____   _____   _____

_____   _____   _____

_____   _____   _____

_____   _____   _____

_____   _____   _____

_____   _____

Words with Many Syllables: Reading IPA

Translate the following multisyllabic words from IPA to English Spelling. The primary stress marks will help. Note the use of elongation marks / : /, extremely weak vowels / ᵊ / and the British style of using / e / in place of / ɛ /.

Taken from Longman's:
These are American variants.

mə 'ræk jʊl əs_____   mɪ nʌsk juːl_____

mɪn ju 'et_____   noʊt ɪf ɪ 'keɪʃ ᵊn_____

nɑːt wɪð 'stænd ɪŋ_____   pen ə 'sɪl ɪn_____

pælə 'miːn oʊ_____   prɪ sɪp ɪ 'teɪʃ ᵊn_____

rɪ gaɪrd ləs_____   səb 'vɝː ʒən_____

sɪŋ kə 'peɪ ʃᵊn_____   'slæp hæp i_____

'wɝːl i bɝːd_____

From Kenyon and Knott:
Note the use of / e / to represent the diphthong / eɪ /.

'kɑrpɛntɚ_____   kɔtərə'zeʃən_____

kærɪktə'rɪstɪk_____   tʃendʒə'bɪlətɪ_____

dɪ 'portmənt_____   dɪsɪn'dʒɛnjʊəs_____

ɛksən'trɪsətɪ_____   ɪlɛktromæg 'nɛtɪk_____

'flɪbɚtɪdʒɪbɪt_____   grædʒʊ 'eʃən_____

From Daniel Jones' Pronouncing Dictionary of the English Language. *(Jones's dictionary gives British pronunciations only):*
Note the use of elongation marks / : / and the British style of using / e / in place of / ɛ / and the British diphthong / aʊ / in place of / oʊ /.

ɪmpləmən'teɪʃn_____   ɪntelɪ 'dʒentsɪə_____

'maɪkrəskəʊp_____   saʊθ 'westən_____

hɪ 'rəʊɪk_____   'hɔɪspaʊə_____

lærɪn'dʒaɪtɪs_____   laɪb'reərɪən_____

me'lɪflʊəs_____   metsəʊsə'prɑɪnəʊ_____

117

Practice Reading IPA

The following transcriptions use pronunciations from *Longman's Pronunciation Dictionary* by JC Wells. Wells gives both British and American pronunciations and more than one pronunciation for each word. Some of the differences in his system from that used in *The Joy of Phonetics and Accents* are: Longman's uses / e / where Colaianni uses / ɛ /; Longman's also adds a tiny schwa sound / ᵊ / between a consonant and / l / or / r /, to create a syllabic l or r. Longman's adds the colon for elongation of certain vowels. For words like saw or call, Longman's uses / ɒ / for American pronunciations and / ɔ / for British . It is important that you are able to adapt to the transcription style used in a given reference. No two dictionaries use phonetics in exactly the same way. It is always wise to consult the pronunciation key to determine the precise transcription style of the work at hand. The following are Longman's' transcriptions of American pronunciations.

/bɑ bɑ blæk ʃip

hæv jʊ eni wʊl

jes sɝ: jes sɝ:

θri bægz fʊl

wʌn fɔɪr maɪ mæstɚ

ænd wʌn fɔɪr maɪ deɪm

ænd wʌn fɔɪr ðə lɪtᵊl bɔɪ

hu lɪvz daʊn ðə leɪn

haɪ dɪdᵊl dɪdᵊl

ðə kæt ænd ðə fɪdᵊl

ðə kaʊ dʒʌmpt oʊvᵊr ðə mun

ðə lɪtᵊl dɒɡ læft tʊ si sʌtʃ spɔɪrt

ænd ðə dɪʃ ræn əweɪ wɪθ ðə spun

dʒæk ænd dʒɪl went ʌp ðə hɪl

tu fetʃ ə peɪl əv wɒɪtᵊr

dʒæk fel daʊn ænd brʊk hɪz kraʊn

ænd dʒɪl keɪm tʌmblɪŋ æftᵊr

hɪkəri dɪkɚri dɑɪk

ðə maʊs ræn ʌp ðə klɑɪk

ðə klɑɪk strʌk wʌn

ðə maʊs ræn daʊn

hɪkəri dɪkəri dɑɪk

ðə nɔɪrθ wɪnd dʌθ bloʊ

ænd wi ʃæl hæv snoʊ

ænd wʌt wɪl pʊᵊr rɑɪbɪn du ðen

pʊᵊr θɪŋ

hiᵊl sɪt ɪn ə bɑɪrn

tʊ   kip   hɪmself   wɔɪrm
ænd   haɪd   hɪz   hed   ʌndᵊr   hɪz   wɪŋ
pʊᵊr   θɪŋ

ðɛᵊr   wʌz   ə   krʊkɪd   mæn   ænd   hi   went   ə   krʊkɪd   maɪˑl
hi   faʊnd   ə   krʊkɪd   sɪkspens   əgenst   ə   krʊkɪd   staɪˑl
hi   bɒɪt   ə   krʊkɪd   kæt   wɪtʃ   kɒt   ə   krʊkɪd   maʊs
ænd   ðeɪ   ɒːl   lɪvd   tʊgeðᵊr   ɪn   ə   lɪtᵊl   krʊkɪd   haʊs /

More Practice Reading IPA

/sʌm   əv   ʌs   ɑːr   bɪkʌmɪŋ   ðə   mɛn   wi   wɑːntɪd   tu   mɛri   glɔːrɪə   staɪnəm/

/jʊᵊr   iðᵊr   paɪᵊrt   əv   ðə   səluːʃᵊn   ɔr   jɔɪr   paɪᵊrt   əv   ðə   prɑbləm   lərɔɪ   ɛldrɪʤ   klivᵊr/

/ɪn   spaɪt   əv   ɛvriθɪŋ   aɪ   stɪl   bɪliv   ðæt   pipᵊl   ɑːr   riːəli   gʊd   æt   haɪrt   æn   fræŋk/

/ɪf   ə   mæn   hæzᵊnt   dɪskʌvᵊrd   sʌmθɪŋ   ðæt   hi   wɪl   daɪ   fɔɪr   hi   ɪzᵊnt   fɪt   tʊ   lɪv   maɪrtɪn   luθᵊr   kɪŋ   ʤunjᵊr/

/hɪstᵊri   wɪl   əbsɑɪlv   mi   fidɛl   kæstroʊ/

/ɪt   eɪnt   oʊvᵊr   tɪl   ɪts   oʊvᵊ   joʊgi   bɛrə/

/tu   sʌm   ɪkstɛnt   ɪf   juv   sin   wʌn   sɪti   slʌm   juv   sin   ðɛm   ɒl   spɪroʊ   ægnu/

/ɪf   ə   fri   səsaɪəti   kænaɪt   hɛlp   ðə   mɛni   hu   ɑːr   pʊᵊr   ɪt   kænat   seɪv   ðə   fjuː   hu   ɑːr   rɪtʃ
                                                ʤaɪn   fɪtsʤerəld   kɛnədi/

/piːpᵊl   hæv   gaɪt   tʊ   noʊ   hwɛðᵊr   ɔɪr   naɪt   ðɛᵊr   prɛzɪdənt   ɪz   ə   krʊk   wɛl   aɪm   naɪt   ə   krʊk
                                                rɪtʃᵊrd   mɪlhaʊs   nɪksᵊn/

/ɪts   dɪfɪkᵊlt   tʊ   bɪliv   ðæt   pipᵊl   ɑːr   staɪrvɪŋ   ɪn   ðɪs   kʌntri   bikɔz   fud   ɪzᵊnt   əveɪləbəl   raɪnəld   reɪgən/

/tɔɪk   loʊ   tɔɪk   sloʊ   ænd   doʊnt   seɪ   tuː   mʌtʃ   ʤaɪn   weɪn/

/ðə   taɪm   tʊ   staɪp   rɛvəluʃᵊn   ɪz   æt   ðə   bɪgɪnɪŋ   naɪt   ði   ɛnd   ædəleɪ   stɪvənsᵊn/

/strɛŋθ   laɪz   naɪt   ɪn   dɪfɛns   bət   ɪn   ətæk   eɪdaɪlf   hɪtlᵊr/

/ɪf aɪd noʊn aɪ wəz goʊɪŋ tʊ lɪv ðɪs lɔːŋ aɪd hæv teɪkən bɛtˑr kɛˑr əv maɪsɛlf   jubi bleɪk/

/ɪn ðə fiˑld əv gʊd wɜ·ld pɑɪləsi aɪ wʊd dedɪkeɪt ðɪs neɪʃˑn tʊ ðə pɑɪləsi əv ðə gʊd neɪbˑr
                                                    fræŋklɪn delɪnoʊ roʊzəvelt/
/noʊ mæn ɪz gʊd ɪnʌf tʊ gʌvˑrn ənʌðˑr mæn wɪðaʊt ðæt ʌðˑrz kənsent   eɪbrəhæm lɪŋkən/

/ɪt ɪz wɛl ðæt wɔːr ɪz soʊ teəˑɪbˑl ɔɪr wi ʃʊd groʊ tuː faɪnd əv ɪt   rɑɪbˑrt edwˑrd li/

Read IPA: British Pronunciations

/ɪf ju lid ə kʌntri laɪk brɪtˑn ju hæv tʊ hæv ə tʌʧ ɒv aɪrəni əbaʊt ju   mɑɪgrət θæʧə/

/ðə mæksɪm ɒv ðə brɪtɪʃ pipˑl ɪz bɪznəs æz juːzuəl sɜ: wɪnstən ʧɜːʧɪl/

/aɪ du nɒt ət ɔɪl rɪzent krɪtɪsɪzəm iːvˑn wen fɔɪ ðə seɪk əv emfəsɪs ɪt fɔɪr ə taɪm pɑɪts kʌmpəni wɪð
riæləti sɜ: wɪnstən ʧɜːʧɪl/

/tu rɪʤɔɪs ɪn laɪf tʊ faɪnd ðə wɜːld bjutɪfəl ænd dɪlaɪtfˑl tʊ lɪv ɪn wəz ə mɑɪk əv ðə grik spɪrɪt wɪʧ
dɪstɪŋgwɪʃt ɪt frɒm ɔɪl ðæt hæd gɒn bɪfɔɪ ɪt ɪz ə vaɪtˑl dɪstɪnkʃən   idɪθ hæməltən/

/nəʊ rɪtˑn lɔɪ hæz evə biːn mɔɪ baɪndɪŋ ðæn ʌnrɪtən kʌstəm spɔɪtɪd baɪ pɒpjʊlərəpɪnjən
                                                    kæri ʧæpmən kæt/

/æn əmerɪkən hæz nəʊ sens ɒv prɪvəsi hi dəz nɒt nəʊ wɒt ɪt minz ðeəɪz nəʊ sʌʧ θɪŋ ɪn ðə kʌntri
                                                    ʤɔɪʤ bənɑɪd ʃɔɪ/

/ɔɪl ðə wɜld əʊvə aɪ wɪl bæk ðə mæsɪz əgeɪnst ðə klɑɪsɪz
                                                    wɪljəm juɪət glædstəʊn/

/ɪf pis kænɒt bi meɪnteɪnd wɪθ ɒnə ɪt ɪz nəʊ lɔɪŋgə pis   lɔɪd ʤɒɪn rʌsəl/

/ɪf aɪ wɜɪræn əmerɪkən æz aɪ æm æn ɪŋglɪʃmən waɪl ə fɔɪrən trup wəz lændəd ɪn maɪ kʌntri aɪ nevə
wʊd leɪ daʊn maɪ ɑɪmz nevə nevə nevə ju kænɒt kɒŋkərəmerɪkə   wɪljəm pɪt/

Writing in IPA: Transcription

The more you write in IPA, the more you will be able to "think" in IPA. It's a bit like learning a new language. There are differences between the spelling of words and their transcription into IPA. The IPA is used to indicate sounds from all languages and all accents. It can even be used to indicate nonsense words or gibberish. It can be used to invent language. It has a more exact symbol-to-sound relationship than the spelling of English. You probably remember learning a number of different rules for sounding out words when you learned to spell. You learned, for example, that the sound / eɪ / could be spelled "ay," "ey," "eigh," or "ai." And that the sound / u / could be spelled "u," "oo," "ough," or "ue," but that sometimes "ough" was / ʌ / as in the word "rough," or / ɔ / as in "cough," or that "oo" could also be / ʊ / as in "foot" or / ʌ / as in "blood." Confusing to a seven-year old, but you did it. Many new ways of teaching reading and writing have been introduced to young students, including phonics (now making a comeback,) the "see and say" method used in the Baby Boomer era, and the i/t/a (initial teaching alphabet.)

Many elementary teachers have used the initial teaching alphabet. In many ways it is similar to the IPA. The i/t/a's special alphabet symbols serve to reform the letter-to-sound irregularities of conventional English spellings. At the other end of the spectrum, the whole language approach deemphasizes phonics in favor of immersion in whole word recognition. Additionally, it downplays the urgency for young children to memorize complicated spelling rules by advocating "invented spellings."

English is a language consisting of words derived from many different languages, each with its own spelling rules. Written IPA is therefore a more accurate representation of the pronunciation of sounds and words. You'll be able to use the IPA to assist you in documenting and recalling a particular choice of pronunciation that you want to use for a given word in a script. In short, using the IPA will be more efficient when what you want to do is communicate the SOUND of a word rather than its spelling.

When you write IPA transcriptions of written English, it will be easier if you get the spelling of the word out of your mind before you try to represent the word in IPA. Our colleague, Pamela Absten, has invented the following "flow chart" for transcribing written English to IPA:

Written Word (See it)
↓
Idea (Picture it in your Mind)
↓
Spoken Word (In your Mouth)
↓
Heard Sounds (In your Ears, in your Body)
↓
Down your Arm onto the Page (Send the Impulse)
↓
Transcribe Phonetics (Write it)

Writing in IPA Using Your Own Accent

In this workbook, we use the IPA in ways for which it was not originally intended. As explained in *The Joy of Phonetics and Accents*, the original use of the IPA was to prescribe precise pronunciations and to set standards for speaking. It was not originally conceived as a way to explore language, as we are doing. In this workbook, you're not being asked to write a definitive, solely correct standard pronunciation of a word. Rather, you are asked to write the phonetic symbols which represent the personal pronunciations of individuals for a particular word. Unless otherwise specified, you should use your own pronunciation of the word, representing your own accent as accurately as possible. As you work in class and in the workbook, you may become aware of differences in pronunciation: between your accent and your teacher's; between your's and your fellow classmates; between your's and a number of dictionary accents. You may even notice inconsistencies in your own accent. Use the IPA as a tool to distinguish your pronunciations from those of others'. Later, you'll use the IPA to acquire other accents, to "take down" or outline a "donor's" accent.

Since you're being asked to use your own pronunciation, you become the authority for the way a word should be pronounced. The buck stops with you. After all, who is the "authority" for the way a word should be pronounced? The English language is full of variations of pronunciation; there are many different accents of American, British , South African and Australian English. A person's accent is influenced by his/her residence, history of residences, parentage, schooling, employment, peer relationships, etc. Remember, your reference for the way you phonetically transcribe a written word should be the way you yourself say it.

Transcribe the following words to IPA using your own accent.

feet _____	fit_____	pray_____
get_____	snap_____	dance_____
first_____	cover_____	up_____
aloud_____	father_____	got_____
old_____	cook_____	you_____
think_____	that_____	jump_____
catch_____	yellow_____	while_____
light_____	crown_____	boil_____

Look at the spellings of these words and transcribe your pronunciation of them. Write the phonetic symbol that corresponds to your pronunciation of each example.

In the word "bee," I pronounce the "ee" _____

In the word "sea," I pronounce the "ea" _____

In the word "priest," I pronounce the "ie" _____

In the word "throw," I pronounce the "ow" _____

In the word "plow," I pronounce the "ow" _____

In the word "palm," I pronounce the "al"_____ (the "l" may be silent)

In the word "soothe," I pronounce the "oo" _____

In the word "prove," I pronounce the "o" _____

In the word "through," I pronounce the "ough" _____

In the word "thorough," I pronounce the "ough" _____

In the word "puff," I pronounce the "ff" _____

In the word "rough," I pronounce the "gh" _____

In the word "thrifty," I pronounce the "th" _____

In the word "bathed," I pronounce the "th" _____

In the word "safety," I pronounce the "s" _____

In the word "pets," I pronounce the "s" _____

In the word "passes," I pronounce the third "s" _____

In the word "phases," I pronounce the second "s" _____

In the word "messages," I pronounce the third "s" _____

In the word "frames," I pronounce the "s" _____

In the word "screams," I pronounce the first "s" _____and the second "s" _____

Transcribing Words in Sentence Context: Weak forms of Words

In conversation, words that express main ideas tend to have prominence, especially nouns and verbs. Prepositions, conjunctions, personal pronouns, articles and auxiliary verbs are usually weak, except where the context calls for contrasting emphasis. (Skinner) The term "weak" refers to less stress in volume, faster tempo, lower pitch, or actual changes in the phonetic sounds. The strong form of a word is the one listed in the dictionary, and is used when the word is stressed. Weak forms help to create the rhythm of speech. We've taken the examples below from Edith Skinner, although she advises against certain of the pronunciations that we have included; a more complete list is found in *Speak With Distinction* (Applause Books, 1992.)

Examples (Skinner):

Word	Strong Form	Weak Form
a	/ eɪ /	/ ə /
an	/ æn /	/ ən /
the	/ ði /, / ðʌ /	/ ðɪ / before a vowel, / ðə / before a consonant
am	/ æm /	/ əm /
can	/ kæn /	/ kən /
was	/ wʌz /, / wɒz /	/ wəz /
some	/ sʌm /	/ səm /, / sm /
to	/ tu /	/ tʊ /, / tə /
at	/ æt /	/ ət /
of	/ ʌv /, / ɒv /	/ əv /
and	/ ænd /	/ ənd /, / ən /
that	/ ðæt /	/ ðət /

 Speak the following sentences using weak forms and transcribe them into IPA.

What are you up to?_____

I'm going to the store._____

I will hear no "buts," young lady._____

I'll go, but I won't enjoy myself._____

Transcribe to IPA the articles, personal pronouns, prepositions, conjunctions and auxiliary verbs in the following speech from *The Undiapered Filefish*, using weak forms where they occur. Write the IPA transcription above the applicable words.

The petite Sirah goes well **with** any lighter dish, **but the** heroic pinot noir is more virile, nearly furry going down, **but a** lifter **of the** spirit **in the** glass. **A** terrible, berry cabernet sauvignon **can** burrow **into the** heroic surrender **and** worry **the** boring chorus **of** chablis drinking conquerors **with** courage **in their** hearts **and on their** tongues. **The** hilarity **of it** all. Not even **a** thought **to the** sauvignon blanc, **which** may perish **if** we tarry **from its** corner **of the** cellar, hidden **behind the** drapery, becoming **a** mirror image **of the** arid land **on which it** thrives.

Transcribe the articles, personal pronouns, prepositions, conjunctions and auxiliary verbs in the following speech from *La Bete*, using weak forms where they occur.

Bejart's   afraid   that   frankness   might   diminish

Our   chances   of   remaining   here   at   court:

He   errantly   presumes   that   you're   the   sort

Who   brooks   no   disagreement   with   his   views,

And   would,   were   his   beliefs   contested,   choose

To   banish   the   offending   opposition
Instead   of   reassessing   his   position.

How   wrong   he   is,   my   lord,   how   very   wrong!

And   that's   what   I've   been   saying   all   along:

The   unembroidered   TRUTH   is   what   you   seek!

Since   no   one   feels   at   liberty   to   speak,

I   therefore   feel   compelled   to   speak   for   *them!*

Transcribe these sentences, from scenes / u /, / ʊ /, / oʊ /, / ɔ /, / ɒ /, / ɑ / of "The Undiapered Filefish" into phonetics, using your own accent. Then compare your transcriptions with those on pages 135 and 136 of this workbook, which contain the authors' transcription of these scenes.

1. It is TRUE, then, that YOU'VE been watching CLUE after CLUE come bristling THROUGH the fog of language,...

_____

_____

2. Where's my GOOD COOK hiding her SUGAR supplies?

_____

3. The WALL had been SCRAWLED on, we're told.

_____

4. WHAT COMEDY, this NOD to the POSSIBLE INVOLVEMENT of GOD is the religion of the ODD COLLEGE SCHOLAR.

_____

_____

Note: Do you make a distinction between / o / and / oʊ /? Distinguish the shorter, unaccented vowel from the diphthong in the following two sentences.

5. I will promise to OBEY if you don't OMIT my OBITUARY.

_____

6. Could you have KNOWN how OLD the TOAST is?

_____

7. I did SPA work in the PLAZA, and found myself among the SUAVEST FATHERS in the town.

_____

_____

Transcribe these sentences from scenes / ʌ /, / ə /, / ɝ / / ɚ / of "The Undiapered Filefish," into IPA using your own accent. Then compare your accent with the pronunciations transcribed on pages 135 and 136 of this workbook, which contain the authors' transcriptions of these scenes.

8. You'll make the HUNK of FUDGE brownies seem like so MUCH JUNK food.

_____

_____

9. I was AMUSED by his ATTEMPT to OBSCURE the filefish involvement, but he was ATTUNED to your mind to APPEAL to that source.

_____

_____

10. HER SIR can INFER the SLUR from five hundred feet, honey.

_____

_____

11. Imagine all the WATER on the JASPER Lane THEATER boards.

_____

_____

Transcribe all of the words in these sentences, from scenes / i /, / ɪ /, / ɛ /, / æ / and / æ / or a / and diphthong scene / eɪ / of "The Undiapered Filefish" into IPA using your own accent. Then compare your pronunciations with those on pages 135 and 136 of this workbook which contain the authors' transcriptions of these scenes.

12. Might WE BELIEVE they are both in NEED of a LEADER, someone WE might BE more readily able to recognize as BEING like a PRIEST?

_____

_____

13. Can I BRING THIS STRING to the PRINCE and RIG a CLIP to SINK HIS GIN?

_____

_____

14. I could put TOGETHER a KETTLE of THEM by FEBRUARY. And we could keep THEM under the BED.

_____

_____

15. MAYBE THEY'LL give us a NAKED scene LATER on.

_____

_____

16. I RANG the LAD, and he used LANGUAGE as though it were AN AX.

_____

_____

17. I'd RATHER BASK in the PATH of my PASTOR than fight a RAFT of NASTY bowls of chowder.

_____

_____

Transcribe these sentences from diphthong scenes / ɔɪ /, / aɪ /, / aʊ / of "The Undiapered Filefish," into IPA using your own accent. Then compare your pronunciations with those on pages 135 and 136 of this workbook, which contain the authors' transcriptions of these scenes.

18. You've got to make a CHOICE, love. Either SPOIL the BOY, or make him a man.

_____

_____

19. He's helped us nab a SLIME taking a BRIBE, he worked with a group of BRINE to bring down the SPY ring in TIGHT pants.

_____

_____

20. The crust in a MOUTH is a HOWL when a CROWN comes loose in a TOWN with no dentist.

_____

_____

Final Y

----What is your final sound in pronouncing words such as "pretty," "likely," "usually," "snappy," and "picky?" Does your pronunciation of the final "y" come closer to your pronunciation of "see," "seat," and "beat?" Or is it close to your pronunciation of "sit," and "kin?" Write the following words in your accent:

USUALLY _____   PICKY _____

SNAPPY _____

Transcribe these sentences, from "Disciplining Dimes," into IPA using your own accent. Then compare your transcriptions with pages 137 and 138 of this workbook, which contain the authors' transcription of these scenes.

1. We have BOOKED an ABSOLUTE RUBE on which we anticipate your IMBIBING.

_____

_____

2. We PAY the bill with a PET canary, or PAT the final bilge with PAP-like fondness.

_____

_____

3. They HAD OBSERVED the DEBT levels which PROVED the DRIVE SAGGED TOWARD DOOM.

_____

_____

4. I can TASTE TATER TOTS BETWEEN my TEETH from LAST evening's sup.

_____

_____

5. The PENGUIN upstarts GROWL about GAWKING at GOD, and you're reduced to calling them coins!

_____

_____

6. COULDN'T you PICK them up?

_____

7. The lead actor had a MOLE, so under stage LAMPS her MOUTH suggested a MOIST MOOD not quite NORMAL.

_____

_____

8. AN OUNCE of PINS AND NEEDLES are worthy of this MOMENT, AND a MONTH of UNHINGED flights of FANCY await our love.

_____

_____

9. SING to me Briggs, get that blasted band to stop BANGING the GONG, and keep the stage cleared.

_____

_____

10. I'll OFFSET THIS LOSS by blinking my MESSAGE to the MESMERIST.

_____

_____

11. I don't want to seem BLASE, but I would prefer HYMNS.

_____

_____

12. My FATHER LEFT it FULL ENOUGH. I'm OFF to FIND the SAFE and FLUFF it back up.

_____

_____

13. I MARVEL at how you SWIVEL in your chair, chain-drinking.

_____

_____

14. The OFFSHOOT is that SHE can SHAKE the OCEAN FISSURE with her TISSUE MACHINE, SHOULD SHE get the nickels to conform to her desires.

_____

_____

15. I want this to be a CASUAL affair, but a VISION of great joy.

_____

_____

16. I THANK heaven for our happiness.

_____

_____

17. ALTHOUGH we feel THE two are SMOTHERING one ANOTHER, BOTHER not THIS delineation THUSLY.

_____

_____

18. I've a HUNCH you could, you WRETCH.

_____

19. This MESSAGE is URGENT.

_____

20. Your SLOW, THISTLE-paced work FILLS my LIFE with an UNCURABLE ULCER, ALTHOUGH it could ALSO be the upshot of ALL that SLAW I've been eating.

_____

_____

_____

21. WON'T you WALLOW WITH me in the WEARINESS of my WANDERING WICKER WASTEBASKET?

_____

_____

22. WHAT is behind the WHITENESS of the WHALE, and did Ahab live with all his faculties?

_____

_____

23. HE was BEHIND us HIDING in the HEATHER, the HEATHEN.

_____

_____

24. RIDE the RAILS with me and we will TRY to REST and RECUPERATE.

_____

_____

_____

25. YOU have got to stop feeding the YAK the JUNGIAN donuts.

_____

_____

Sentences from "The Undiapered Filefish," transcribed into phonetics.

Compare your own transcriptions with some of those found in Kenyon and Knott's *A Pronouncing Dictionary of American English*. In several cases, two choices of transcription are offered. If you want to be particularly accurate in your understanding of the Kenyon and Knott pronunciations, consult their introduction. They often give several pronunciations of a word. Note that Kenyon and Knott use / e / and / o / where *The Joy of Phonetics, JC Wells* and *Daniel Jones* use / eɪ / and / oʊ /.

1./ ɪt ɪz tru ðɛn ðæt juv bɪn wɑtʃɪŋ klu æftɚ klu kʌm brɪslɪŋ θru ðə fɑg əv læŋgwɪʤ /

2. / wɛrz maɪ gʊd kʊk haɪdɪŋ hɝ ʃʊgɚ səplaɪz /

3. / ðə wɔl hæd bɪn skrɔld ɑn wɪr told /

4. / wʌt kɑmədɪ ðɪs nɑd tʊ ðə pɑsɪbl ɪnvɑlvmənt əv gɑd ɪz ðə rɪlɪʤən əv ðɪ ɑd kɑlɪʤ skɑlɚ /

/ wʌt kɒmədɪ ðɪs nɒd tʊ ðə pɒsɪbl ɪnvɒlvmənt əv gʊd ɪz ðə rɪlɪʤən əv ðɪ ɒd kɒlɪʤ skɒlɚ /

5. / aɪ wɪl prɑmɪs tʊ obe ɪf jʊ dont omɪt maɪ obɪtʃʊɛrɪ /

/ aɪ wɪl prɒmɪs tʊ obeɪ ɪf jʊ doʊnt omɪt maɪ obɪtʃʊɛrɪ /

6. / kʊd ju hæv non haʊ old ðə tost ɪz /

7. / aɪ dɪd spɑ wɝk æt ðə plɑzə ænd faʊnd maɪsɛlf əmʌŋ ðə swɑvəst fɑðɚz ɪn taʊn /

8. / jul mek ðə hʌŋk əv fʌʤ braʊnɪz sim laɪk so mʌtʃ ʤʌŋk fud /

9. / aɪ wʌz əmjuzd baɪ hɪz ətɛmpt tʊ əbskjʊr ðə faɪlfɪʃ ɪnvɑlvmənt bət hi wəz ətund tʊ jʊr maɪnd tʊ əpɪl tʊ ðæt sɔrs /

10. / hɝ sɝ kæn ɪnfɝ ðə slɝ frəm faɪv hʌndrəd fit hʌnɪ /

11. / ɪmæʤɪn ɔl ðə wɔtɚ ɑn ðə ʤæspɚ len θɪətɚ bɔrdz /

135

12. / maɪt wi bɪliv ðe ɑr boθ ɪn nid əv ə lidɚ sʌmwʌn wi maɪt bi mɔr rɛdɪlɪ ebl tʊ rɛkɪgnaɪz æz biɪŋ laɪk ə prist /

13. / kæn aɪ brɪŋ ðɪs strɪŋ tʊ ðə prɪns ænd rɪg ə klɪp tʊ sɪŋk hɪz ʤɪn /

14. / aɪ kʊd pʊt tʊgɛðɚ ə kɛtl əv ðɛm baɪ fɛbrʊɛrɪ ænd wi kʊd kip ðɛm ʌndɚ ðə bɛd /

15. / mebi ðel gɪv ʌs ə nekɪd sin letɚ ɑn /

16. / aɪ ræŋ ðə læd ænd hi juzd læŋgwɪʤ æz ðo ɪt wɝ æn æks /

17. / aɪd ræðɚ bæsk ɪn ðə pæθ əv maɪ pæstɚ ðən faɪt ə ræft əv næstɪ bolz əv ʧaʊdɚ /

   / aɪd raðɚ bask ɪn ðə paθ əv maɪ pastɚ ðən faɪt ə raft əv nastɪ bolz əv ʧaʊdɚ /

18./ juv gɑt tʊ mek ə ʧɔɪs lʌv aɪðɚ spɔɪl ðə bɔɪ ɔr mek hɪm ə mæn /

19./ hiz hɛlpt ʌs næb ə slaɪm tekɪŋ ə braɪb hi wɝkt wɪð ə grup əv braɪn tʊ brɪŋ daʊn ðə spaɪ rɪŋ ɪn taɪt pænts

20. / ðə krʌst ɪn ə maʊθ ɪz ə haʊl wɛn ə kraʊn kʌmz lus ɪn ə taʊn wɪð no dɛntɪst /

Sentences from "Disciplining Dimes," transcribed into phonetics.

1. / wi hæv bʊkt æn æbsəlut rub ɑn wɪʧ wi æntɪsɪpet jʊr ɪmbaɪbɪŋ /

2. / wi pe ðə bɪl wɪθ ə pɛt kənɛrɪ ɔr pæt ðə faɪnəl bɪlʤ wɪθ pæplaɪk fɑndnəs /

3. / ðe hæd əbsɝvd ðə dɛt lɛvlz wɪʧ pruvd ðə draɪv sægd tɔrd dum /

4. / aɪ kæn test tetɚ tɑts bɪtwin maɪ tiθ frʌm læst naɪts sʌp /

5. / ðə pɛngwɪn ʌpstɑrts graʊl əbaʊt gokɪŋ æt gɑd ænd jʊr rɪdust tʊ kɔlɪŋ ðɛm kɔɪnz /

6. / kʊdnt ju pɪk ðɛm ʌp /

136

7. / ðə lid æktɚ hæd ə mol so ʌndɚ stɛʤ læmps hɚ mavθ səgʤɛstəd ə mɔɪst mud nat kwaɪt nɔrməl /

8. / æn avns əv pɪnz ænd nidlz ɑr wɚ·ði əv ðɪs momənt ænd ə mʌnθ əv ʌnhɪnʤd flaɪts əv fænsɪ əwet avr lʌv /

9. / sɪŋ tv mi brɪgz gɛt ðæt blæstɪd bænd tv stap bæŋɪŋ ðə gaŋ ænd kip ðə stɛʤ klɪrd /

10. / aɪl ɔfsɛt ðɪs lɔs baɪ blɪŋkɪŋ maɪ mɛsɪʤ tv ðə mɛzmərɪst /

11. / aɪ dont want tv sim blaze bət aɪ wvd prɪfɚ hɪmz /

12. / maɪ faðɚ lɛft ɪt fvl ɪnʌf aɪm ɔf tv faɪnd ðə sef ænd flʌf ɪt bæk ʌp /

13. / aɪ marvəl æt hav ju swɪvəl ɪn jvr ʧɛr ʧɛndrɪŋkɪŋ /

14. / ði ɔfʃut ɪz ðæt ʃi kæn ʃek ði oʃən fɪʃɚ wɪθ hɚ tɪʃu məʃin ʃvd ʃi gɛt ðə nɪklz tv kənfɔrm tv hɚ dɪzaɪrz /

15. / aɪ want ðɪs tv bi ə kæʒvəl əfɛr bət ə vɪʒən əv gret ʤɔɪ /

16. / aɪ θæŋk hɛvən fɔr avr hæpɪnɛs /

17. / ɔlðo wi fil ðə tu ɑr smʌðɚɪŋ wʌn ənʌðɚ baðɚ nat ðɪs ðɪlɪnɪɛʃən ðʌslɪ /

18. / aɪv ə hʌnʧ ju kvd ju rɛʧ /

19. / ðɪs mɛsəʤ ɪz ɚ·ʤnt /

20. / jvr slo θɪsəl pest wɚk fɪlz maɪ laɪf wɪð æn ʌnkjvrəbl ʌlsɚ ɔlðo ɪt kvd ɔlso bi ði ʌpʃat əv ɔl ðə slo aɪv bɪn itɪŋ /

21. / wont ju walo wɪθ mi ɪn ðə wɪrɪnəs əv maɪ wandɚɪŋ wɪkɚ westbæskɪt /

137

22. / hwʌt ɪz bɪhaɪnd ðə hwaɪtnəs əv ðə hwel ænd dɪd ehæb lɪv wɪð ɔl hɪz fækəltiz /

23. / hi wəz bɪhaɪnd ʌs haɪdɪŋ ɪn ðə hɛðɚ ðə hɪðən /

24. / raɪd ðə relz wɪθ mi ænd wɪ wɪl traɪ tʊ rɛst ænd rɪkupəret /

25. / ju hæv gɑt tʊ stɑp fidɪŋ ðə jæk jʊŋɪən donʌts /

Transcribing Syllabic Sounds / n /, / l / , / m /, / r /

A syllabic consonant is one which is used in place of a vowel, usually in an unstressed syllable. Syllabic / n / sometimes takes the place of / ən / in unstressed syllables. Examples, with IPA spellings from Kenyon and Knott, are:

/ rizn /   / bekn /   / hæpn /   / prɪzn /   / maʊntn /   / ʤɛtɪsn /   / rɛtəsnt /   / sɛdntɛrɪ /   / sʌdnlɪ /

Transcribe the following words to IPA.

EDEN_____   DIDN'T_____

FLORESCENCE_____   HEAVEN_____

Transcribe the following words (which do not contain syllabic / n /.)

PLAN_____   MIDNIGHT_____

Syllabic / l / sometimes takes the place of / əl / in unstressed syllables. Examples are:

/ pipl /   / sæmpl /   / trʌbl /   / hwɪsl /   / rɪvɝ·səbl /

Transcribe the following words using the syllabic / l / to IPA.

NOODLE_____   DELECTIBLE_____

PARTICLE_____   HOSTILE_____

Transcribe the following words (which do not contain syllabic / l /.)

REAL_____   STEALTH _____

Syllabic / m / occurs less frequently. It sometimes takes the place of / əm /, such as / ælbm / or / spæzm /.

Transcribe the following words (which do not contain syllabic / m /.)

FEMALE_____   TRAMPOLINE _____

STEAM _____   SEAMLESS_____

Syllabic / r / sometimes takes the place of / ɚ / in unstressed syllables. Examples are / faðr /, / aktr /.

Transcribe the following words using syllabic / r /.

CREATOR_____   THEATER_____

PERPETUAL_____   SEER_____

In *Longman's Pronunciation Dictionary,* J.C. Wells states that "any nasal or liquid in a syllable in which there is no other vowel must automatically be syllabic." Thus, / r / is included in Longman's syllabic consonants for the American pronunciations which are indicated in other systems as / ɚ /. Where Kenyon and Knott use / ɚ /, Longman's uses   / r / or / ᵊr / to show that the syllabic "r" is preferred. Daniel Jones' *English Pronouncing Dictionary* (for British Enlgish) also uses syllabic / n / , /1 /, and / r /. Both Longman's and Jones sometimes use an italicized schwa before the consonant (or a tiny schwa) to indicate a preference for the syllabic consonant.

Kenyon and Knott	Longman's (American)	Jones
kʊdnt	kʊdᵊnt	kʊdnt
mɑrmled	mɑːrm ə leɪd	mɑːməleɪd or mɑːmleɪd
spæzəm	spæz ᵃm (italicized schwa)	spæz ᵃm (italicized schwa)
sʌfɚ	sʌfᵊr	sʌfɔ
kaʊnsl	kaʊn sᵊl	kaʊnsl
ɪmɛʒrəbl	ɪ meʒ ər əb ᵊl	ɪ meʒərəbl
pɑvɚti	pɑː vᵊrt i	pɒvəti
pɑzətɪvɪzəm	pɑːz ət ɪv ɪz ᵃm (italicized schwa)	pɒzɪtɪvɪzəm (italicized schwa)

Transcribe the following words into IPA. Use the phonetic symbols that most accurately represent your own pronunciation of the words.

Portugal_____   cracker_____   wouldn't_____

practical_____   mother_____   didn't_____

future_____   penetration_____   frazzled_____

poodle_____   smitten_____   activism_____

The Personal/Partner Accent Project

In order to distinguish the subtle nuances of your own pronunciations from those of others, it will be useful for you to team up with someone. You will be pursuing two simultaneous objectives in this exercise: learning to distinguish your own accent from others' and listening to and analyzing a partner's accent.

Find a partner in your class whose accent is somewhat different from your own. The contrasts between your accent and those of your classmates may be so subtle that no obvious choice of partner presents itself. If this is the case, you can consider the following questions when searching for a partner: which members of your class come from a different part of the country, or the world than you do? Which classmates are from different ethnic and cultural backgrounds? Which of your classmates come from urban? suburban? rural backgrounds? Each of these considerations can have an influence on the accent in which someone speaks.

Your classmates may come from different countries, different regions of the same country or different cities. There are countless accents in each English-speaking country; each can be divided into several geographic segments; for example, you can break down the US into several geographic segments based on the speaking style of the inhabitants: New England, East Coast, South, Midwest, Northwest, Southwest, and West Coast. Your first job is to determine which region you come from and which classmates come from other regions. If your hearing is acute, you will be able to discern pronunciation contrasts within these regions; pronunciations vary from state to state, province to province and city to city within the large regions. There are also other variables which determine accent. Rural accents are often distinguishable from urban accents. Some accents are culturally defined; some are defined by social class. There are many influences on pronunciation; choices for pronunciation go in and out of "style." Not all African Americans speak in a "Black Dialect," nor do all Latino Americans speak with a Latino accent. Not all Londoners speak the same; and many people who do not actually belong to a specific culture, class or race have adopted many of the distinguishing pronunciations of a culture which is not the one they were "born into."

The Personal/Partner Accent Project is actually a project about *idiolects*. An idiolect is not the general dialect of a region but the personal accent of an individual. An idiolect may therefore have many identifiable regional traits but will also reflect the unique accent of the individual. You must distill some of the more prominent characteristics of your partner's speech in order to represent his/her accent. When you create a character for theatre, you must also narrow down the accent features you wish to include. In creating a character, you want to capture the essence of a believable "person" not just a set of characteristics. Therefore, when you create a dialect, you need more than one donor to be able to distinguish *personal* characteristics from regional or class characteristics. For this project, allow yourself the freedom to observe and then to exaggerate elements of your partner's rhythm, melody, resonance qualities and physicality in order to more fully capture the essence of the person. It is often uncomfortable to see and hear ourselves represented by other people, whether they are accurate or not. Make an agreement with your partner that you will allow her the freedom to imitate and exaggerate, but to do so with sensitivity.

General Description of Your Partner's Accent

Observe your partner's behavior when she is not aware you are doing so. Observe her while she is speaking to others. Note postural and gestural characteristics, which may be useful to you in imitating your partner's accent. Physical characteristics are often reflected in a person's speech--in their rhythms, tempi, emphasis, etc. Observe your partner's face and note how he moves his eyes, his forehead, his cheeks, his neck. Especially note how he uses his lips: are his lips tense? Does he use his top lip to speak? Does he use less or more lip-rounding than you do? Does he smile a lot? Does he hold his breath while listening or before speaking? Does he press his lips together after speaking a sentence? Describe the general characteristics you have observed. Also note any overall characteristics that are descriptive of your partner's speech, such as strong nasality, frequent glottal shocks or hard attacks, overall clarity lack of clarity, etc.

PRONUNCIATION

Phonetic Elements

1. Review the section in *The Joy of Phonetics and Accents* on "Accents" (pages 67-125.) Also, review your repertory of phonetic symbols.

2. Make a tape recording of your partner in conversation, telling a story and reading key words and sentences. The tape recording will allow you to focus on your partner's speech without visual input.

3. Do a "background information" session (page 83, *The Joy of Phonetics and Accents*) with your partner.

4. Use the list of "sound contrasts"on pages 83-85 of *The Joy of Phonetics and Accent*s. Also, use the lists of words on pages 86-96 and 74-77. With your partner, read the paired words out loud. Compare your pronunciations. Use the accent outline chart on pages 147 to 150 of this workbook, to "take down" your own pronunciations and those of your partner. When you each use the same sound, but in slightly different ways, use nuance markings (see page 143 of this workbook) to express these differences. Instead of reading the words in isolation, which may make you sound over-careful and artificial, try to use them in the context of conversation.

5. For listening to specific sounds in sentence context, use the plays "The Undiapered Filefish" and "Disciplining Dimes" in *The Joy of Phonetics and Accents*.

6. Review the lists of nuance markings throughout the "Accents" chapter of *The Joy of Phonetics and Accents* and in this chapter in the workbook. Use nuance markings whenever they can aid in your distinguishing your accent from your partner's. If you find yourself using one nuance marking repeatedly, such as the marking for extra nasality on vowels, choose to make that a regular feature of the accent rather than marking nasality on all of the vowels. If, on the other hand, nasality only occurs in certain situations or on certain vowels, use the nuance marking.

7. Observe your partner. Note the way he/she uses his/her body. Note your partner's physical rhythms, gestures, posture, breathing. Which of these features can you use to capture the essence of your partner? Referring to the Accent Outline Chart, converse with your partner using the key words. Take time to transcribe the differences between your accent and your partner's accent, so that when you refer to the chart later on, you will be able to reproduce both pronunciations.

THE LILT OF THE ACCENT

Melodic Elements

1. Review the material on pages 96-98 of *The Joy of Phonetics and Accents* regarding pitch, drift, inflections and intervals.

2. Listen to your partner while focusing solely on the melody.

3. Sing the melody of your partner's speech. Write the melody on paper, using either a musical staff or just dots in space indicating relative progressive pitches. Or write the words in space as on page 97 of *The Joy of Phonetics and Accents*.

4. Compare the melodic characteristics to your own speech so that you can distinguish differences between you and your partner. Note any particular melodies your partner uses habitually.

Rhythmic Elements

1. Review the material on pages 98-99 of *The Joy of Phonetics and Accents* regarding rhythm.

2. Listen to your partner's speech while focusing on the rhythm--the pattern of beats or stresses, the tempi, the changes in tempi. You'll be able to find physical cues in your partner's habitual movements, breath and gestures as well as by listening in isolation.

3. Play the rhythm of your partner's speech, perhaps by tapping it. Write the rhythm using musical notes, dots and dashes or by using nuance markings for length as indicated on pages 98-99 of *The Joy of Phonetics and Accents*.

4. Compare the rhythmic characteristics to your own speech. Note any rhythms your partner uses habitually.

Resonance Characteristics (Quality)

Some resonance characteristics may be a feature of accent or dialect. Many dialect methods refer to the "point of focus" for the dialect or the "place the voice seems to be coming from." David Alan Stern uses this concept on his tapes, "Acting with an Accent." It will be useful for you to imagine where your partner's voice may be coming from--whether it is further back in the mouth or further forward, whether your partner seems to be speaking from lower or higher in his/her body than you do. Vocal quality is determined by the particular combination of resonances a person habitually uses. Some people use very little nasal resonance, some use predominantly nasal resonance. Some people use primarily lower pharyngeal ("chest") resonance with very little "head" resonance, etc. Vocal quality is sometimes referred to as "breathy, strident, nasal, denasal, harsh, rough, hollow, rotund,"etc. It is likely that your quality differs from your partner's, so it is useful to compare.

Variations in Vowels: Nuance Markings

Often you will hear a small difference between your pronunciation of a vowel sound and that of another person. The difference will be enough for you to distinguish, but not enough to indicate a completely different phonetic symbol. You may then want to represent the difference with a nuance marking. These markings and variations will be useful to you in distinguishing among subtle differences in vowels. Speak each example changing your pronunciation to reflect the change suggested by the nuance marking. In this workbook, nuance markings appear to the right of the affected symbol.

Extra nasality:	~	as in / fræ˜ ŋk /
Extra elongation:	:	as in / pli: z /
A higher tongue position:	ˌ	as in / kæˌθ /
A lower tongue position:	ˍ	as in / pɛˍn /
Extra lip rounding:	ˌ	as in / muˌn /
Extra lip widening or stretching:	ͨ	as in / siͨ /
Breathiness :	..	as in / stoʊ.. v /
Vowel between / I / and / i /:	ɨ	as in / prɪtɨ /

Variations in consonants

De-voicing (for a usually-voiced consonant):	˳	as in / slæb˳ /
Voicing (for a usually unvoiced consonant):	˯	as in / p˯rɪtɪ /
Dentalized sound:	˯	as in / prɪtˍɪ /
Glottal stop	ʔ	as in / maʊnʔn /

PERSONAL/PARTNER ACCENT PROJECT
PARTNER PROFILE

GENERAL DESCRIPTION OF MY PARTNER'S ACCENT:

DESCRIPTION OF THE QUALITY (RESONANCE CHARACTERISTICS) OF PARTNER'S VOICE:

DESCRIPTION OF PITCH CHARACTERISTICS OF PARTNER'S ACCENT:

DESCRIPTION OF RHYTHM CHARACTERISTICS OF PARTNER'S ACCENT:

LISTING OF SPECIAL PRONUNCIATIONS OF SPECIFIC WORDS (IN IPA:)

My Pronunciations   My Partner's Pronunciations

_____   _____

_____   _____

_____   _____

_____   _____

_____   _____

_____   _____

_____   _____

_____   _____

_____   _____

_____   _____

_____   _____

ACCENT OUTLINE CHART
VOWELS

Phonetic Symbol	Key Word	Key Word in My Accent	Key Word in My Partner's Accent
i	_____	_____	_____
ɪ	_____	_____	_____
eɪ	_____	_____	_____
ɛ	_____	_____	_____
æ	_____	_____	_____
'Variable A' æ or ɑ (as in the word ask)	_____	_____	_____
ɑ	_____	_____	_____
ə	_____	_____	_____
ʌ	_____	_____	_____
ɚ	_____	_____	_____
ɝ	_____	_____	_____
'Variable O' ɒ or ɑ (as in the word odd)	_____	_____	_____
ɔ	_____	_____	_____
oʊ	_____	_____	_____
ʊ	_____	_____	_____
u	_____	_____	_____
aɪ	_____	_____	_____
ɔɪ	_____	_____	_____
aʊ	_____	_____	_____
ju	_____	_____	_____

ACCENT OUTLINE CHART
DIPHTHONGS

Phonetic Symbol	Key Word	Key Word in My Accent	Key Word in My Partner's Accent
ɪɚ	_____	_____	_____
ɛɚ	_____	_____	_____
ɑɚ	_____	_____	_____
ɔɚ	_____	_____	_____
ʊɚ	_____	_____	_____
aɪɚ	_____	_____	_____
ɔɪɚ	_____	_____	_____
aʊɚ	_____	_____	_____

ACCENT OUTLINE CHART
CONSONANTS

Phonetic Symbol	Key Word	Key Word in My Accent	Key Word in My Partner's Accent
b	_____	_____	_____
p	_____	_____	_____
g	_____	_____	_____
k	_____	_____	_____
d	_____	_____	_____
t	_____	_____	_____
v	_____	_____	_____
f	_____	_____	_____
z	_____	_____	_____
s	_____	_____	_____
ʒ	_____	_____	_____
ʃ	_____	_____	_____
ð	_____	_____	_____
θ	_____	_____	_____
ʤ	_____	_____	_____
ʧ	_____	_____	_____
h	_____	_____	_____
j	_____	_____	_____
l	_____	_____	_____
m	_____	_____	_____
n	_____	_____	_____

ŋ   _____   _____   _____

r   _____   _____   _____

w   _____   _____   _____

hw   _____   _____   _____

Dialects and Accents for Stage and Film

Accent is one aspect of character. In creating a role, accent is one of the areas of work an actor must do. Just as you would research an unfamiliar aspect of a character's life (a particular handicap, a vocation, a life perspective, etc.) you must research the accent or dialect.

There are many instructional resources for dialects and accents in the forms of tapes and books. However, these materials are only as useful as they are accurate, specific and appropriate to your needs. Obviously, the better your research materials, the more prepared you'll be for the demands of the role. Some materials are prepared by dialect and accent experts, and are well-designed for instruction. Some tapes are of primary sources--speakers from a particular geographical region, what we call "accent donors"--and some tapes are of teachers demonstrating accents. Ideally, the best materials would include several primary source speakers from the exact region of your character, with step-by-step instructions describing the way to achieve the accent; the instructor would know you, your accent and your best learning style. In this way, the teaching would be tailored specifically to you. Even better would be several videos of primary-source speakers (donors) that are "just like" your character. More likely, however, you'll find recordings that are too general for your character, or too dated for the period of the play, or tapes with instructions, but no primary-source speakers. You should know where to find the materials that are commercially available, so that when you need them you won't be in a panic. Beyond that, you should have the skills to create a dialect or accent for yourself from primary source speakers -- "donors."

Your ability to work with the IPA plus your awareness of the phonemic characteristics of your own accent are the preliminary tools you need. The next step is a skill you learned in Acting 101--Observation. If you were to create a dialect or accent for a region, you would need to acquire audio recordings and/or videotapes of several different people from that region, observe and analyze each one's speech, then distill the accent down to several of the salient characteristics of that accent. It is often helpful to combine "donor" research with commercially-available tapes and materials. It is more accurate to have more than one perspective. The Accent-Donor Project is one of many steps in preparing an "accent" role.

The Accent-Donor Project

(Use the following material after re-reading the accent donor project section of *The Joy of Phonetics and Accents* pages. 78-99).

Interviewer_____

Recording Date_____

Accent or Dialect of Donor_____

SUGGESTIONS FOR THE INTERVIEW SESSION

To Prepare For the Interview:
       *Choose a relatively private, quiet space
       *Check that you have good tape recorder, blank cassette tape,
       batteries or power cord
       *Check the volume level of interviewee's voice and adjust
       recording level
       *Bring sheets with sentences and paragraphs for interviewee
       to read aloud

1. General get-acquainted conversation. 5 minutes
       *Be sure to record: Alphabet A-Z
                     Numbers 1-20, 30, 40, 50, 60, 70, 80, 90, 100
                     The Days of the Week, Months of the Year
       *Some place names/locations of native area: towns, rivers,
       cities, etc. (Bring a world atlas or map if possible)
       *Unusual slang or casual names for things or places

2. Gather information from donor. 5 minutes

Information to Gather
       Age_____
       Education_____
       Work/Occupation/Avocation_____
       Birthplace_____

Family Origins
       Parents' Native Languages_____

                     _____

       Parents' Places of Birth and Upbringing_____

                     _____

       Parents Vocations_____

                     _____

Acquisition of English

     At What Age_____
     From Whom (American, British?)_____
     How (Schools, Classes, Conversation?)_____

3. Ask your donor to read word lists and sentences from the vowel and consonant plays in *The Joy of Phonetics and Accents*, or other prepared material which surveys the sounds of English. These will allow dialects to be compared to one another. Coach them to read slowly. 5 minutes

4. *Questions to engage donor in longer period of speaking.* Coach your donor to speak freely about several subjects or events of interest. This will allow you to note more of the melodic and rhythmic aspects of the dialect. 20-30 minutes

Suggestions:
--tell about funny or touching event from childhood
--talk about favorite holiday (food, games, customs, gifts)
--talk about special event in their life (marriage, births, moves, travel)
--subject they feel strongly about
--a story about a friend or relative
--sing a folk song or children's song
--recite joke, poem or prayer

5. After you have finished the 30-40 minute session, have your donor speak a few lines from a play which is appropriate to their accent.

**Note any special phrases or expressions in their casual speech: surprise, affection, frustration, exclamation, etc.

**The entire tape should be 30 to 40 minutes. Make sure your own speaking is minimal on the tape. It might help to remind them that you want to record *their* voice and that you will tell them about yourself *after* the taping.

Objectives for this project:
1. To learn a process for acquiring and using native speakers for stage accents and dialects.
2. To practice the process of interviewing "donors."
3. To practice transcribing the accent in IPA, notating the specific substitutions as they differ from your own pronunciations.
4. To practice describing the lilt of the accent. This includes specific pitch, rhythm and resonance features.
5. To practice applying the accent to an appropriate text, adjusting the accent to the rhythms of the text.
6. To increase your own range of expression--the rhythmic, melodic and resonance features of your speech and your choices for pronunciations.
7. To become even more familiar with the specific features of your accent so that your pronunciation choices are conscious rather than merely habitual.

In choosing your donors, keep these criteria in mind:
1. Choose someone with an accent that is different than your own.
2. Choose someone whose accent you find interesting and distinctive.
3. Choose someone who will agree to converse openly with you rather than someone who is shy about being taped.
4. Choose people with different ages and vocations from your own.
5. Keep in mind characters for which the donor's accent would be appropriate.
6. Choose someone whose speech has characterisitcs of one area rather than someone who has moved around a great deal and has "lost" their accent.

ACCENT DONOR PROJECT
ACCENT PROFILE

BACKGROUND INFORMATION ON DONOR AND COUNTRY/REGION:

DESCRIPTION OF PRONUNCIATION FEATURES OF DONOR'S ACCENT:

LILT CHARACTERISTICS

1. DESCRIPTION OF THE QUALITY (RESONANCE CHARACTERISTICS) OF DONOR'S VOICE:

----

2. DESCRIPTION OF PITCH CHARACTERISTICS OF DONOR'S ACCENT:

----

3. DESCRIPTION OF RHYTHM CHARACTERISTICS OF DONOR'S ACCENT:

ACCENT DONOR CHART

Donor's Name_____   Donor's Country/Region_____

VOWELS

Phonetic Symbol	Key Word	Key Word in My Accent	Key Word in My Partner's Accent
i	_____	_____	_____
ɪ	_____	_____	_____
eɪ	_____	_____	_____
ɛ	_____	_____	_____
æ	_____	_____	_____
'Variable A' æ or ɑ (in words like ASK)	_____	_____	_____
ɑ	_____	_____	_____
ə	_____	_____	_____
ʌ	_____	_____	_____
ɚ	_____	_____	_____
ɝ	_____	_____	_____
'Variable O' ɒ or ɑ (in words like ODD)	_____	_____	_____
ɔ	_____	_____	_____
oʊ	_____	_____	_____
ʊ	_____	_____	_____
u	_____	_____	_____
aɪ	_____	_____	_____
ɔɪ	_____	_____	_____
aʊ	_____	_____	_____
ju	_____	_____	_____

ACCENT DONOR CHART

Donor's Name_____ Donor's Country/Region_____

DIPHTHONGS

Phonetic Symbol	Key Word	Key Word in My Accent	Key Word in My Partner's Accent
ɪɚ	_____	_____	_____
ɛɚ	_____	_____	_____
ɑɚ	_____	_____	_____
ɔɚ	_____	_____	_____
ʊɚ	_____	_____	_____
aɪɚ	_____	_____	_____
ɔɪɚ	_____	_____	_____
aʊɚ	_____	_____	_____

ACCENT DONOR CHART

Donor's Name_____ Donor's Country/Region_____

CONSONANTS

Phonetic Symbol	Key Word	Key Word in My Accent	Key Word in My Partner's Accent
b	_____	_____	_____
p	_____	_____	_____
g	_____	_____	_____
k	_____	_____	_____
d	_____	_____	_____
t	_____	_____	_____
v	_____	_____	_____
f	_____	_____	_____
z	_____	_____	_____
s	_____	_____	_____
ʒ	_____	_____	_____
ʃ	_____	_____	_____
ð	_____	_____	_____
θ	_____	_____	_____
dʒ	_____	_____	_____
tʃ	_____	_____	_____
h	_____	_____	_____
j	_____	_____	_____
l	_____	_____	_____
m	_____	_____	_____
n	_____	_____	_____

ŋ   _____   _____   _____

r   _____   _____   _____

w   _____   _____   _____

hw   _____   _____   _____

Appendix One: The 'Variable A,' in words such as ASK.

The words below are typically pronounced with the 'short A' sound / æ / in US speech. In southern England, they are typically pronounced with the 'broad A' / ɑ /. We call words of this type 'Variable A' words. These words can be identified by spelling. As a rule, words spelled with the letter 'A' followed by one of the following consonant combinations belong to the 'variable A' category: AFT; ANCE; ANT; AST; AND; ANS; ASK; APH; AFF; ANCH; ATH; AVS; ASS; ASP; AMP. This rule is complicated by the fact that there are many exceptions to it. For instance, the word CLASS, belongs to the 'variable A' category and is pronounced with the 'broad A' in southern British speech, and the 'short A' in US speech , but, the word MASS, although it is spelled with the same ASS ending, is pronounced with the 'short A' sound in both southern British and US speech. If there is a reason for such exceptions, it is something that only phonologists would understand. In order to minimize confusion over 'variable A' words, a comprehensive list is given below. If a word is on this list, it is pronounced with the 'broad A' sound in a southern British accent, and the 'short A' sound in a US accent. The list below is sub-divided into groups of words with like endings. For instance, all words to which this rule applies which have ASK endings are grouped together, as are words with AMP; ATH; ANCH endings, etc.

This list of words has been compiled by comparing pronunciation entries in Kenyon and Knott, Daniel Jones, JC Wells and Webster's Rhyming Dictionary. Speech teacher Edith Skinner's manual, <u>Speak With Distinction</u>, contains a similar, although not identical list of words, which she calls the 'ASK LIST.' Skinner's 'ASK LIST' is given in strict alphabetical order, rather than by word endings. It is the hope of the present authors that organization by word endings will clarify which words belong on the list and which do not, as well as providing a handy reference.

Remember, there are exceptions to the 'variable A' rule. If a word does not occur in the following lists, assume that it is not in the 'Variable A' category and is typically pronounced with the 'short A' in both southern British and US speech.

Note: In some parts of New England and Canada, you will hear 'variable A' words pronounced with the 'intermediate A' sound / a /, however, this pronunciation is comparatively rare. On the other hand, in parts of the British Isles, such as Ireland, the 'intermediate A' pronunciation of 'Variable A' words is extremely common. The practice of using the 'intermediate A' in the pronunciation of 'variable A words' in the American classical theater is considered old-fashioned today.

AFT Spellings:

abaft	graft	thereafter	France	**ANT spellings:**
aft	grafts	thereinafter	Frances	aslant
after	grafted	turboshaft	Francis	aunt
afterbirth	grafter	understaff	free-lance	aunts
afterbrain	grafting	understaffed	free-lanced	auntie
afterdamp	handcraft	waft	free-lances	aunties
after-dinner	handicraft	wafts	free-lancer	can't *(but not CAN*
aftereffect	handicrafted	waftage	free-lancers	*or CANT)*
afterglow	handicrafting	wafted	free-laning	chant
afterimage	handicrafter	wafting	glance	chanted
afterlife	Hovercraft	watercraft	glanced	chanter
aftermath	indraft	witchcraft	glancer	chantey
aftermost	indraught	woodcraft	glances	chanties
afternoon	indraughts		glancing	chanting
aftertaste	indraughted		glancingly	chantries
afterward	kraft		happenchance	chantry
afterwards	Kraft	**ANCE & ANS**	Hopdance	chianti
afterword	Krafft	**spellings:**	lance	disenchant
antiaircraft	laugh	advance	lanced	disenchanted
campercraft	laughs	advancer	lances	disenchantedly
camshaft	laughing	answer	Lancet	disenchanting
countershaft	laughter	answered	lancet	displant
craft	overdraft	answers	lancets	eggplant
crafted	overdrafts	answerable	lancing	enchant
crafts	overdrafted	answerably	mischance	enchanted
crafty	overdrafting	answering	mischances	enchantedly
craftier	paragraph	chance	mooncalf	enchanter
craftiest	paragraphed	chanced	overglance	enchanting
craftiness	paragraphing	chancing	overglanced	enchantment
craftily	quaff	chancey	overglances	enchantress
crankshaft	quaffed	chancier	overglancing	enchants
daft	quaffing	chaniest	perchance	explant
dafter	raft	chancel	prance	Grant
daftest	rafted	chancels	pranced	grant
daftly	rafter	chancelry	Prancer	granted
daftness	raftered	chancelries	prancer	granter
draft	rafting	chancellor	prances	granting
drafted	rockshaft	chancellors	prancing	grantor
drafts	rotorcraft	chancer	ropedancer	grants
drafting	scoutcraft	chancies	trance	houseplant
drafter	seacraft	country-dance	trances	implant
draught	shaft	Dance		implanted
draughts	shafts	dance		implanting
draughted	Shaftsbury	danced		implants
draghting	spacecraft	dancer		interplant
draughty	staffed	dances		plant
draughtier	staffing	dancing		planted
draughtiest	stagecraft	enhance		planter
engraft	statecraft	enhanced		plants
engrafts	taft	enhancing		plaster
engrafted	tafted	entrance (verb)		
engrafting	telegraph	entrances (verb)		
engraftment	telegraphed	entranced (verb)		
	telegraphing	entrancedly		
		entrancing (verb)		

preplant
replant
shan't
slant
slanted
slanting
slantingly
slantwise
supplant
supplanted
supplanting
transplant
transplantable
transplanted
transplanting
vantage
vantages

AST spellings:
aghast
alabaster
avast
blast
blasted
blastie
blasting
blasts
cast
castaway
caste
castes
casted
caster
casting
castoff
castoffs
Castor
castor
castor-oil
disaster
disasters
disasterous
disasterouly
fast
fasted
fasting
fastness
flabbergast
flabbergasted
flabbergasting

forecast
forecasted
forecaster
forecasters
forecasting
forecasts
ghastly
ghastlier
ghastliest
ghastliness
last
lasted
lasting
lastingly
lastly
mast
masted
master
masterful
masterfully
mastering
masterpeice
mastery
masthead
masting
nasty
nastier
nastiest
nastily
nastiness
outcast
outcasted
outcasting
outcasts
outlast
outlasted
outlasting
outlasts
past
past-master
past-masters
Pasteur
Pasteurize
passtime
passtimes
pastor
pastors
pastoral
pastorals
pasture
pastures

pastured
pasturing
plaster
plastered
plasterer
plastering
plasters
recast
repasture
steadfast
steadfastly
steadfastness
stedfast
telecast
telecasts
topmast
topmasts
upcast
upcasts
vast
vaster
vastest
vastness
vasty

AND spellings:
Chandler
chandler
chandlers
command
commanded
commands
commander
commanders
commanding
commandment
commandments
commando
countermand
countermanded
countermanding
demand
demands
demanded
demander
demanders
demanding
Hopdance
reprimand

reprimanded
reprimander
reprimanders
reprimanding

ASK spellings:
ask
asked
asker
askers
asking
bask
basked
basker
baskers
basket
basketball
basketry
basking
Bergomask
cask
casked
casket
caskets
casking
casks
flask
flasks
mascara
mask
masked
masking
masks
masque
masques
overtask
overtasked
overtasking
overtasks
pass-key
rascal
rascalities
rascality
rascally
rascals
task
tasked
tasking
taskmaster
taskmasters

taskmistress
taskmistresses
tasks
unmask
unmasked
unmasking
unmasker
unmasks
wastebasket

APH, AFF, ALF & AUGH spellings:
calf
calf-skin
calf's
calf's-foot
chaff
chaffed
chaffer ('one who chaffs,' but not the verb, 'to chaffer.')
chaffing
chaffingly
chaffless
chaffy
distaff
epigraph
epigraphs
epitaph
Falstaff
graph
graphed
graphing
graphs
half
Halfcan
Halfmoon
laugh
laughable
laughed
laugher
laughing
laughingly
laughter
mooncalf
paragraph
paragraphed
paragrapher

paragraphing
paragraphs
quaff* (*this word
and its other forms
are commonly
pronounced with
/ ɑ / in both
southern British and
general American).
quaffed*
quaffer*
quaffing*
quaffs*
staff
staffed
staffer
staffing
staffs
telegraph
telegraphed
telegraphing
telegraphs

ALV spellings:
calve
calved
calves
calving
halve
halved
halves
halving
salve
salved
salves
salving

ASS spellings:
brass
brassie
brassy
brassier
brassiest
class
classed
classer
classier

classiest
classiness
classy
glass
glassed
glasses
glassful
glassier
glassiest
glasily
glassy
Grasmere
grass
grassed
grasses
grassier
grassiest
grassy
outclass
outclassed
outclasses
outclassing
pass
pass-book
pass-key
pass-word
passable
passably
passed
passes
passel
passer** (**'one
who passes,' not the
ornithological term).
passers
passers-by
passing
passman
passmen
Passover
Passovers
passport
passports
passtime
passtimes
passwoman
passwomen
repass
repassed
repasses
repassing

surpass
surpassed
surpasses
surpassing
surpassingly
trespass
trespassed
trespasser
trespasser
trespassing
unsurpassed

ASP spellings:
clasp
clasped
clasping
clasps
enclasp
enclasped
enclasping
enclasps
gasp
gasped
gasper
gasping
gaspingly
gasps
grasp
grasper
grasped
grasping
graspingly
grasps
hasp
hasped
hasping
hasps
passport
passports
rasp
raspberry
raspberries
rasped
raspiness
rasps
raspy

AMP spellings:
counterexample
ensample
ensampled
ensampling
example
exampled
examples
exampling
sample
sampled
sampler
samples
sampling

ATH spellings:
bath
bath-brick
bath-chair
bathhouse
bathroom
baths
bathtub
bathtubs
birdbath
bypath
footbath
footpath
lath
lather
lathy
path
pathfinder
pathfinders
pathless
pathway
pathways
towpaths
wrath*** (*** This
word and its other
forms is commonly
pronounced with
/ æ / in general
American and / ɒ /
in southern British).
wrathful***
wrathfully***

Appendix Two: The 'Variable O' sound.

The following is a list of words spelled with the letter O, such as LONG and ODD, for which it is difficult to provide a single rule for pronunciation. We refer to these words as 'Variable O' words. The vowel in such words is considered 'unstable,' meaning that it can be pronounced in a variety of equally acceptable and inteligible ways. (See page 58 of *The Joy of Phonetics and Accents* for more information about unstable vowels).

Depending on regional and cultural influences, pronunciation of the vowel in 'Variable O' words ranges from / ɔ /, to / ɑ /, to / ɒ /.

This list contains two sub-categries of 'Variable O' words, they are:

1)Words such as LONG, which have three common pronunciations in the US: / lɔŋ /, / lɒŋ / and / lɑŋ /. Words of this type appear in the list followed by an asterisk.

2)Words such as ODD, which have two common pronunciations in the US: / ɑd /, and / ɒd /. Words of this type appear in the list without an asterisk.

Additionally, there are words in this list which are spelled with WA, such as WASH. The vowel in these words is commonly pronounced in the US in the same two variations as the vowel in the word ODD: / wɑʃ /, and / wɒʃ/. WA words also appear in the list without an asterisk.

The point of this list is not to prescribe a preferred way of speaking these words on the stage. It is rather, to provide the student with an awareness of a spelling-based category of words, which will enhance the student's ability to analyze and assimilate regional and foreign accents for the stage.

A-bomb	amoral*	bakeshop	blouson	bouillon
Aaonic	Amoric*	Balmoral*	blue-collar	box
abdominal	amphipod	bandbox	bluebottle	boxer
Abercrombie	anabolic	bandog*	Bob	boxers
abolish	anacoluthon	Bankok	bob	boxy
abominable	anaconda	barbershop	bobbin	boycott
abscond	analog	Baroque (British RP)	bobble	boycotts
absconder	analogue	baryon	Bobby	boycotter
absolve	anaphoric*	baton	bobby	boycotters
accost*	androgenous	bebop	bock	Boz
Acheron	androgeny	bedrock	bod	breechblock
acknowledge	anomaly	beechdrops	bodge	brioche
acock	anon	beef Stroganoff*	Bodger	broadcloth*
across*	anthropic	befog	bodger	Brock
ad hoc	antibody	begot	bodice	brock
add-on	antiknock	begotten	body	brolly
Adolphus	antilog	bellhop	boffo	bronc
adopt	anybody (British RP)	belong*	bog	bronco
Aelolic	apalogue	belonging*	bogged	brontosaurus
aeon	aplomb	belongings*	boggy	broth*
Aesop	Apollo	bergamot	Bolingbroke	brothel
Aesopian	apologue	benthos	bomb	brush-off*
Aesopic	apostle	besot	bonbon	Brythonic
aforest*	apostolic	betatron	bond	bubonic
aftershock	apothecary	betroth	bonder	buckshot
Agamemnon	apple-polish	betrothal	bonfire	bucolic
agelong*	apricot	better-off*	bong	bulldog*
agitprop	apriority*	beyond	bonkers	bullfrog
agog	achctcctonic	biathlon	Bonner	bullshot
agon	archon	big-shot	bookshop	burdock
agone	argon	billycock	boondocks	busybody
agonic	aristocracy	bionic	bop	butterscotch
ahistorical*	Aristophanes	bionics	bopped	buttstock
aileron	arthropod	bipod	bopper	bygone
Ailoth	ascot	bird-dog*	Boris*	Byronic
airdrop	asyndeton	bird-watch	boron*	cabachon
albatross*	atop	blackcock	borrow	cachalot
alcohol*	aurochs	blacktop	bosh	cachepot
alcoholic*	authority*	blast-off*	Bosnia	caisson
aleatoric*	Avalon	blesbok	boson	Calgon
aliquot	awash	blob	boss*	caloric*
allegorical*	axon	blobs	bossy	Camelot
allegorist*	bawcock	bloc	Boston	cannot (when the accent is on the first syllable).
allegory*	Babylon	block	Bostonian	
allot	backblock	blond	botch	canonic
allotter	backblocks	bloodshot	bother	canorous*
aloft*	backdrop	bloodstock	Bothnia	Havelock
along*	backlog	blot	Bothwell	havelock
alpenstock	backstop	blotch	bottle	capon
Amazon	backwash	blotter	bottom	carbolic
amnion		blotto	botulism	

carbolic
carbonic
carhop
carillon
carry-on
carring-on
carryings-on
carryon
cartographer
cartography
cartop
catabolic
catalog
catalogue
catatonic
categorical*
celedon
cephalopod
chaconne
chameleonic
chatterbox
cheesecloth*
Chekov*
cheongsam
Cheops
chiffon
chignon
Chobham
chock
chockablock
chocolate*
choler
Cholly
chomp
Chomsky
chon
chondroma
chop
chop-chop
chopped
chopper
choral*
choreographer
choreography
choric*
chorion
chorus*
chrestomathy
Christoph*
Christopherson
chromotography

chronic
chthonic
cinematography
cleoptera
clip-on
clitoric*
clock
clod
cloddy
clodhopper
clog
cloggy
clomp
clonk
clop
clopped
close-cropped
clot
cloth*
cloths*
clotted
co-opt
cob
cobble
cobbled
cobby
cock
cocky
cod
coddle
coddling
codger
codify
codon
codswallop
coffee*
coffeepot*
coffin*
cog
cognate
cognizance
cognomen
congoscenti
cohost
coin-op
coldcock
coleopterous
colic
Coliseum
collar
college

collet
collie
collop
colly
Colly
colophon
colossal
colossus
column
come-on
comedy
comet
comment
comp
comparable
compass
con
conch
concocter
condor
condy
confident
conglomerate
Congo
conic
conk
conkers
Conna
Connacht
connate
Connaught
connectivity
Connolly
Connor
Connors
Conor
conquer
Conrad
conscience
consequence
consequent
conservation
conservationism
conservationist
conserve (when the first syllable is accented)
Consett
Considine
consignee
consolation

console (when the first syllable is accented)
consolidate
consomme
consonance
consonant
consort
conspecific
constant
convent
convolve
cooling-off*
cop
cops
copper
copra
copse
copt
copulate
coracle*
coral
cordon*
Corin*
Corinth*
corncob
coronation
coronets
cor*respond
cosh
cosmic
cosmonaut
cosmopolitan
cosmos
cost*
Costa Rica
Costain
costard
Costard
cost*ermonger
cot
cottage
cotter
cotton
cough*
coulomb
coupon
Covent Garden (British RP and sometimes General American)

Coventry
cox
crackpot
cradlesong*
crampon
crayon
cretonne
criss-cross*
crock
crocket
Crockett
crockpot
Croft*
Cromwell
crop
crops
cropped
cropper
cross*
crotch
crouton
cryonic
crytron
culotte
cumquat
cutoff
cyclonic
cyclops
cyclotron
Dacron
dashpot
dead-on
deadlock
deathwatch
decagon
defog
deforest
defrock
demagogue
demagogy
demigod
demijohn
demimondaine
demimonde
demob
democracy
demolish
demonic
demonstrative
deplorable*
desktop

despond	do*ggone	drophead	epiphenomenon	floral*
despot	do*ggoned	dropkick	epoch	Florence*
deuteron	do*ggonedest	dropleaf	epoxide	florid*
Deuteronomy	doggy*	droplet	epoxy	Florida*
devolve	doghouse*	dropped	epsilon	Florimel*
dewdrop	dogleg*	dropper	equinox	florin*
diabolic	doglegged*	dropping	erelong*	florist*
diachronic	dogma*	dropsical	erogenous	Florizel*
dialogue	dogmatic*	dropsy	Eros	floss*
diamonic	dogmatism	dropwart	escallop (British	flossed*
diatom	dogmatist*	drosky	RP)	flossy*
diatonic	do*gwatch	drosphilia	estop	flotsam
dingdong	doll	dross	Ethiop	flowerpot
diphthong*	dollar	dry dock	Ethiopic	flyswatter
dismbody	dollop	dry-shod	etymon	fob
disharmonic	dolly	Dubonnet	euphonic	fodder
dishcloth*	dolor	dugong	euphoric*	fog
dishonest	dolorous	Dunlop	Eurodollar	foggy
dishonor	dolphin	duologue	evensong*	folkorist*
dissolvable	domicile	dysphonic	everybody (British	follicle
dissolve	dominant	dysphoric*	RP)	follow
divebomb	don	eardrop	evolvable	follow-on
dobbin	Don Juan	earshot	evolve	folly
doc	dong	eavesdrop	exon	fond
docile	donkey	eavesdropper	explorer*	Fong
dock	doorknob	echelon	exteriority*	footstop
docket	doorstop	eclogue	eyedropper	fop
doctor	Doppler	ectopic	eyeshot	forage*
Dodd	Doric*	eggnog	eyewash	foray*
dodder	Doricles*	electron	facecloth*	foregone
doddering	Doris*	electronic	faceoff*	forehead*
dodge	Dornoch*	electroshock	falloff*	foreign*
dodger	Dorothea*	electronic	far-gone	foreknowledge
Dodgson	Dorothy*	elevon	far-off*	forelock
dodgy	Dorrit*	elongate*	fatstock	forest*
doff*	Dos Passos	embody	feedstock	foretop
dog-catcher*	DOS	embolic	fermion	forgot
dog-eared*	doss	emboss*	fetlock	forgotten
dog-eat-dog*	dosser	embossable*	filet mignon	fossil
dog-fight	dossier	embossed*	firebomb	Foster*
dog*	dot	embrionic	firebox	foster*
dog*	dotter	en bloc	firedog*	fox
Dogberry*	dotterel	end-stopped	flattop	fox-trot
dogcart*	dottle	endlong*	fleshpot	foxy
dogend*	dotty	ensconce	flintlock	Freon
dogfish*	doublecross*	eon	flip-flop	freon
dogfood*	doxy	ephod	flock	frisson
dogger*	draconic	epiglottal	flog	frock
doggerel*	dreadlocks	epiglottis	flop	frog
doggie*	drop	epilogue	flopped	frolic
doggo*	dro*p-off	epiphenomenal	flopper	from (British RP)

frond
frost*
froth*
Frothingham*
furlong*
fusspot
gallipot
galosh
gamecock
garrote
garroter
garrotes
garroting
garrottes
garrotting
gastropod
gavote
gearbox
gemsbok
geopolitics
glob
globby
globetrotter
glop
gloss*
gloss*
glossal*
glossary*
glossed*
glossy*
glottal
Gloucester
gluon
gnocchi
gnomic
gnomon
gob
gobble
gobbles
Gobbo
God
Gods
Goddess
Goddesses
godfather
goings-on
Golconda
goldenrod
golf
golliwog
golly

Gond
gondola
gone
goner
gonfalon
gong
gong
goof-off*
Gorringe*
gosh
gosling
got
Gotham
Gothic
Goths
gotten
gouache
Gough (variant)
gourmond
grapeshot
grasshopper
gridlock
grog
groggy
grommet
Grosz
grot
grotto
groundhog
guillemot
gumdrop
gunshot
gyrocompass
gyroscopic
H-bomb
hadron
hands-off*
hangdog*
hardtop
harmonic
have-not
Havelock
haycock
Haycock
hayloft*
headlock
headlong*
headstock
headstrong*
hearthrob
hedgehog

hedgehop
hedgehopped
hedgehopper
hedonic
hegemonic
helicon
Hellespont
hemlock
heptagon
hereof (British RP)
heterodox
heterodoxy
heterogeny
hexagon
hexapod
hilltop
historic*
historical*
histrionic*
hoar-frost*
hob
Hobbes
hobble
hobby
hobnob
hock
hocks
hockey
hockshop
hod
hodgepodge
Hodges
Hoffman
Hofstra
hog
hogwash
holiday
Holland
holler
hollow
holly
hollyhock
holocaust
homebody
homily
homogenize
homogenized
homogenous
homologue
homonym
homophonic

Honda
honest
Hong Kong
honk
honker
honkie
honkytonk
Honolulu
honor
hop
Hopalo*ng
hopped
Hopper
hopscotch
Horace*
horology
horoscope*
Horowitz*
horrible*
horrid*
Horrocks*
horror*
hospice
hospitable
hostel
hostile
hot
hot-rod
hot-rodder
hotbox
Hotchkiss
hotchpot
hotdog*
hotly
hotshot
Hottentot
hotter
Hoxton
hydroponic
hyperbolic
hypnagogic
hypocrisy
icebox
icon
ideologue
ill-gotten
immoral*
impossible
imposter
improper
incorrigible*

innominate
intercom
intercross*
interferon
interlock
intoxicate
involve
ionic
ironic
isogloss*
isoglossal*
isosceles
isotonic
jabberwocky
jack-in-the-box
jackpot
job
jobs
jock
jockey
jocund
jodhpurs
Joffrey
jog
John
jolly
jonquils
Josh
josh
Joshua
jostle
jot
jukebox
jump-off*
kabob
kaleidoscopic
kampong
kaon
kapok
Karloff*
kibosh
kick-off*
kickoff*
kilowatt
knob
knobby
knock
knocks
Knopf
knot
knots

knotter
knotting
knowledge
Knox
kolkhoz
Kong
Kongo
krypton
kumquat
kyrie eleison
laconic
lacrosse*
lactonic
Lancelot
Laocoon
lapdog*
Launcelot (general American)
layoff*
Leacock
leadoff*
leapfrog
lepton
lexicon
liaison
life long*
lift-off*
limacon
livelong*
livestock
lob
lobby
loblolly
lock
Locke
locket
locks
lodge
lodger
loft*
Loft*
log
loincloth*
loll
lolling
lollipop
lollop
lolly
Lombardy
long*
longing*

longer*
longest*
lo*ng shot
long*
Long*
Lonny
lop
lopped
lopper
loquat
lorgnon
lorry*
loss*
lost*
lot
lotto
lox
lozenge
macaronic
Macedon
Macintosh
mackintosh
macron
mailbox
majority*
malaprop
manioc
marathon
marathoner
mascot
Masonic
mastodon
matchbox
matchlock
McIntosh
megawatt
melancholic
melancholy
Memnon
menthol*
meritocracy
mesencephalon
meson
metabolic
microdot
micron
microscopic
microscopy
milksop
Minnetonka
minority*

misanthropic
misbegotten
misogynist
mnemonic
mob
mobster
mock
mod
modder
model
moderate
modicum
modify
module
Moffat
Mogg
moll
mollify
molly
mollycoddle
mom
Monaco
Monadnock
monadnock
monaural
Mongolic
mongrel
monitor
monocotyledon
monogyny
monologue
monphonic
monsters
Montana
monthlong*
mop
mopped
mopper
moral*
Morris*
morrow*
Moslem
moss*
mossy*
moth*
moths*
motley
motmot
motocross*
motorcross*
Mott

motte (British RP)
mottes
mottle
motto
moufflon
mouflon
mountaintop
mouthwash
moxie
muon
musquash
muttonchops
myrmidon
mystagogue
nabob
namedrop
namedropper
neologism
neon
neoned
nephrotomy
neuron
neutron
Niger-Congo
nightlong*
Nimrod
nob
nobble
nobby
nobody (British RP)
nock
nod
nodder
noddle
Noddy
noddy
nodule
nog
noggin
nominal
nominate
non
non-profit
nonagon
nonce
nonchalance
noncom
nonny
nonstop
Norris*
nosh

not
notch
noumenon
noxious
nozzle
nucleon
nylon
oarlock
obelisk
Oberon
object
oblo*ng
obol
obsequies
obsolete
obvious
Occident
Occidental
occupy
ocelot
octagon
octet
odd
odder
oddity
odds-on
odyssey
of (Brithish RP)
off*
offal*
office*
Office*
officer*
Officer*
oft*
often*
Ogden*
oilcloth*
Oliver
Ollie
omelette
omicron
ominous
on
one-off*
ontogeny
onyx
Oolong*
oolong*
op
opera

Appendix 2 "variable O"

opposite

opt

optical

opulent

oracle*

oral*

orange*

orator*

oratorical*

oratory*

Or*egon

oriface*

origin*

orisins*

Orlon

orotund*

orris

orthodox*

orthodoxy

Oshkosh

Osmond

Osric

ossify

ostinato

Ostrogoth

Ostrogothic

Othello *(also / o/)*

Ott

otter

Otto

out-of-pocket

outcrop

outcross*

outfox

overtop

Ovid

ovulate

ox

oxen

oxy

oxymoron

Oz

Ozzie

o'clock

O'Connell

O'Conner

padlock

pantheon

papillon

parabolic

paradox

paragon

paraquat

Paraquat

parasol*

paregoric*

part-song*

Parthenon

parton

paternoster

Paternoster

patriotic

pawnshop

pay-off*

peacock

peacocks

peasecod

pedagogic

pedagogue

pedegogy

Pelops

pelorus*

Pentecost*

Pentecostal*

pentagon

peon

Pequot

Percheron

peridot

periscopic

permafrost*

Peron

pettifog

Phaethon

phantasmagoric*

phenom

phenomena

phenomenal

phenomenon

philanthropic

Philharmonic

philosophy

Phlegethon

phlox

phon

phonic

phonics

phosphor

phosphoric

phosphorus

photography

photographer

photon

phylloxera

pibroch

pick-off*

pickpocket

pillar-box

pillbox

ping-pong

Ping-pong

pion

piton

plainsong*

planktonic

platonic

playoff*

plethoric*

plod

plodder

plonk

plonked

plop

plopped

plot

plotter

plutocracy

plutonic

pock

pocket

pod

podgy

pogrom

polish

politic

polka dot

pollywog

polyglot

polygon

polyp

polyphonic

pomp

Pompey

pompom

pompon

pompous

ponce

pond

ponder

poniard

pop

poplar

popper

Poppy

poppy

poppycock

popular

populate

pornography

porridge*

porringer*

posh

positron

posse

possible

post hoc

postbox

posteriority

posterity

pot

pother

Potsdam

potshot

pottage

potter

poverty

pox

predominant

prehistoric*

priority*

probably

proboscics

process

proctor

prod

profit

prog

progeny

prognosticate

progress

prolegomenon

prologue

prolong*

prom

prominent

prong

prop

proper

property

prophet

propped

propper

prosatic

proselytize

Proserpine

prosody

prospect

prosper

prosper

Prospero

Prosser

prostaglandin

prostate

prostatectomy

prosthesis

prostitue

prostitution

prostrate

prostration

prothalamion

proton

provenance

provender

Providence

providence

provident

province

provocation

proxy

put-off*

put-on

put-upon

pylon

pyloric*

python

quad

quadraphonic

quadraphonics

quadrophonic

quaff

quaffed

quaffing

quag *(variant)*

quaggy *(variant)*

quahog

qualm

qualms

quarantine*

quarrel*

quarreled*

quarreler*

quarreling*

quarried

quarry*

quash

quashed
quasi
quad
quod
radiosonde
radon
raindrop
rainwash
rakeoff*
ramrod
rayon
red-hot
redox
reforest*
remodel
resolvable
resolve
resolved
resolving
respond
responded
responder
responding
response
restorative*
retro-rocket
revolvable
revolve
revolved
revolver
revolving
rhebok
rhetoricial*
rhomb
rhomboid
ringtoss*
rip-off*
ripstop
roadblock
Rob
rob
robbed
robber
robbery
Robert
Robin
robbing
robot
robs
roc
rock

rocked
rocker
rocking
rocket
Rocky
rocky
Rod
rod
Rodger
Roger
roger
rollick
rollicked
rollicker
rollicking
Romanoff*
romp
romped
romper
Ron
Ronald
rooftop
rooftops
rootstock
Rosiland
Ross*
roster
rostrum
rot
rotted
rotten
rotter
rotting
Roth*
Rothamsted
Rothay
Rothbury
Rothenstein
Rother
Rotherfield
Rotherham
Rotherhithe
Rothermere*
Rothersthorpe
Rotherwick
Rothes
Rothesay
Rothko
Rotham
Rothschild*
Rothwell

roughshod
rowlock
Roz
Rubicon
run-on
run-off*
sackcloth*
sailcloth*
salon
saltbox
sandlot
sansculotte
sardonic
sardonyx
sarong*
Sasquatch
sawed-off*
schlock
schlocky
schnorrer*
schnozzle
schnozzola
scholar
schottische
Schottky
scoff*
sconce
Scot
Scotch
scotch
scrod
scrofula
scrofulous
Scuppernong
seadog*
sell-off*
semilog
semiology
semiotic
semitropical
send-off*
seniority*
septention
set-off*
sexpot
shadowbox
shaggy-dog*
shallot (when
accented on second
syllable)
shalom (British RP)

shamrock
sharecrop
sharecropper
sheepdog*
sheetrock
Sherlock
shishkabob
shishkabobs
shock
shocked
shocking
shocks
shod
shoddy
shog
shone (British RP)
shop
shops
shopped
shopper
shoppers
shopping
shortstop
shot
shott
show-off*
showstopper
shutoff*
shuttlecock
Shylock
sidelong*
silicon
sine qua non
singalong*
singsong*
Sinological
Sinologist
Sinologue
sitcom
Siwash
skibob
skyrocket
Slavonic
sling-shot
slip-knot
slip-on
slipshod
slipslop
slob
slobs
slog

slogged
slogging
slogs
slop
slopped
sloppy
slops
slosh
sloshed
slot
sloth* (variant)
smallpox
smock
smog
smoggy
Smollet
Snap-on
snapshot
snob
snobbery
snobby
Snodgrass
snog
snot
snowdrop
snuffbox
so-long*
sob
sobbed
sobbing
sock
socked
socket
sockets
Socrates
sod
soddy
Sodom
sodomy
soffit
soft*
soften*
softer*
softest*
soggy
Sol
solder
solemn
solemn
solid
solitary

Solomon
Solomons
Solon
solon
solvable
solve
solved
solving
somber
somebody *(British RP)*
somewhat *(British RP)*
sonde
sondes
song*
songs*
sonic
sono*rity
sonorous
sop
sophomore
sophomoric
sorrel*
sorrier*
sorriest*
sorrow*
sorrowful*
sorry*
sot
souchong*
soupcon
soursop
sovran
spatterdock
spermatazoon
spin-off*
splosh
splotch
splott
Spock
sporran*
spot
spotted
spotter
spotting
spotty
Springbok
springbok
sprocket
squab

squabble
squabs
squad
squads
squalid
squalor
squander
squash
squashed
squashing
squat
squatted
squatter
squatting
stand-off*
stand-offish*
stand-offishly*
stand-offishness*
starcrossed*
steenbok
stereophonic
stereoscopic
stethoscopic
stink-bomb
stock
stockpot
stocky
stodge
stodged
stodges
stodgy
stolid
stollon
stomp
stomped
stomper
stomping
stonecrop
stop
stopcock
stopped
stopper
stopping
stopwatch
Stroganoff*
strong*
strong*box
stronger*
strop
suave
sub-dominant

subatomic
subplot
subtonic
sunspot
superiority*
supersonic
supersonics
swab
swabbed
swabber
swabbing
swabs
swaddle
swaddling
swaddy
Swadlincote
Swaffer
Swaffham
Swaffield
swallow
swallowed
swallowing
swallowtail
swamp
swamped
swampland
swamps
swampy
swan
swan-upping
Swanage
Swanee
Swanley
Swann
swanned
swanning
swans
swansdown
Swansea
Swanson
swan so*ng
Swanton
Swanwick
swan'sdown
swap
swapmeet
swapped
swapper
swapping
swaps
swash

swashbuckler
swashbucklers
swashbuckling
swashed
swashes
swastika
swastikas
Swat
swat
swatch
swatches
swath
swat
swatted
swatter
swatters
swatting
swats
sweatshop
sweetshop
swob
swop
swot
swots
symbolic
symphonic
synagogue
synchronic
synod
systolic
tablecloth*
tablecloths*
Tagalog *(variant)*
tagalong*
take-off*
talkathon
tampon
tap-off*
tarok
taxon
taxonomist
taxonomy
teapot
teardrop
technocracy
tectonic
tectonics
teenybopper
teeter-totter
Teflon
telamon

telecom
telephonic
telescopic
telethon
Teutonic
theocracy
theodicy
theodolite
theogeny
theological
theomachy
theomancy
theopagy
Theophilus
Theophist
Theosophical
Theosophy
thereof *(British RP)*
thereon *(British RP)*
thereupon *(British RP)*
Thermopylae
Thessalonica
thingamabob
thingamabobs
Thom
Thomas
Thommie
thon
thong*
throb
throbbed
throbbing
throbs
Throckmorton
thrombotic
thrombus
throng*
throngs*
throstle
throttle
throttled
throttled
ticktock
Ticonderoga
tie-on
tinderbox
tip-off*
toboggan
Tocharian
Tocqueville

tocsin · Tomsk · topographer · trade-off* · ultrasonic
tod · tomtit · topographic · tragicomedy · unclod
Todd · tong* · topography · travelogue · uncross*
toddle · Tonga · topologist · triceratops · undercroft*
toddler · Tongan · topology · trigonometry · underdog*
toddling · Tonge · Topolsky · trioxide · undergone
toddy · tong · toponym · tripod · undershot
Todhunter · tongs* · topos · tripos · unheard-of (British
Todman · tonic · topped · Triton · RP)
Todmorden · tonics · Topper · Trocadero · unorthodox
toff · Tonnintoul · topper · trod · unstop
toffee* · Tonka · Topping · trogon · unstopped
toffy* · Tonkin · topping · trolley · unstopping
toft* · Tonks · topple · trolleybus · upon
tog · toneau · tops · trollop · upshot
toggle · Tonnie · topsail · Trollope · upsilon
Tokharian · tonsil · Topsham · trombone · vagabond
tolerable · tonsilectomy · topside · trombones · Vietcong
tolerant · tonsilitis · Topsider · trombonist · virion
tolerate · tonsorial · topsoil · tromp · Virol
toleration · tonsure · topspin · trompe l' oeil · Visigoth
Tollmache · tonsuring · Topsy · tromped · Visigothic
Tolpuddle · tontine · topsy-turvy · tromping · vitrolic
Toltec · Tonto · Torcross* · Trondheim · volcano
Tolu · Tonypandy · Tordoff* · trophic · volley
Tolene · toolbox · toric* · tropic · volume
Tolworth · top · torrefaction* · tropics · volunteer
Tom · top-down · torrefy* · tropopause · volvox
tom · top-dress · Torremolinos* · troppo · vomit
tom-cat · top-flight · Torrence* · trot · Von
tom-tom · top-heavy · Torrens* · troth (general · wabble
tomahawk · top-level · torrent* · American) · wad
Tomalin · top-notch · Torres* · Trotsky · wadded
tombola · top-secret · torrid* · Trotskyist · Waddell
tomboy · top-spin · tosh · Trotskyite · wadder
tomfool · top-up · toss* · Trott · Waddeson
tomfoolery · Topcliffe · toss-up* · trotted · wadding
Tomkins · topcoat · tossed* · trotter · Waddington
Tomkinson · topcro*ss · to*sspot · trotting · waddle
Tomlin · topgallant · tot · Trottiscliffe · Waddon
Tomlinson · Topham · Tothill · try-on · waddy
Tommie · topic · Totley · turboprop · wadge
Tommy · topical · Totnes · turn-cock · wadi
tommy · topicalize · Tottenham · turn-off* · Wadsworth
tommyrot · topknot · totter · turn-on · waffle
tomorrow* · Toplady · Totteridge · twaddle · Wagga
Tompion · topless · tottery · twas (British RP) · wainscot
Tompkin · topmast · Totton · twat · Walachia*
Tompkins · topmost · towmond · twats · Walampur*
Tompkinson · topnotch · toxic · Typhon · Walberswick*
Toms · topo · toyshop · typhonic · Walcott*

Walden*	wandering	washed-up	Watkin	wombat
Waldo*	wanderings	washer	Watkins	wonky
Waldorf*	wanderlust	washer-dryer	Watkinson	Won Ton
Walford*	wanders	washer-woman	Watling	wonton
walk-on	Wandles	washerly	Watney	woodcock
Walla	wanigan	washer-man	WATS	wop
wallaby	wanly	washes	Watson	workaholic
Wallace	wanness	washhouse	Watt	workbox
Wallachia*	Wansbeck	washing	watt	workshop
wallah	Wanstead	washing-up	watt-hour	wot
Wallasey	Wansworth	Washington	wattage	wristwatch
wallet	want	Washington	Watteau	write-off*
walliker	want	Washingtonian	wattle	wrong*
Wallingford*	Wantage	washleather	wattlebird	wroth*
Wallington*	Wantagh	washman	Watts	Wyandot
Wallis	wanted	washmen	wearthercock	Wyandotte
Walloon	wanting	washout	wedlock	xenon
wallop	wants	washrag	well-off*	Xerox
wallop	wapentake	washroom	well-thought-of	yearlong*
wallow	wapiti	washstand	(British RP)	yellow-dog*
wallow	Wapner	washtub	what (British RP)	yob
Wallwork*	Wapping	washwoman	whatnot (British RP)	yod
Wally*	Wappinger Falls	washwomen	wherefrom (British RP)	Yom Kippur
Walmer*	warlock	washy	whereof (British RP)	yon
Walney*	warrant*	wasn't (British RP)	whereon (British RP)	yond
walrus*	warren*	wasp*		yonder
Walsall*	warrent*	wasp-waisted*	whereupon (British RP)	Yonkers
Walsh*	warrentee*	wassail		Yorick*
Walsham*	warrentor*	wast	whistle-stop	Yoruba*
Walshingham*	Warrington*	Wastdale	white-collar	zircon
Walt*	warrior*	Wastwa*ter	white-hot	zirconic
Walter*	Warriss*	Wat	whitewash	Zoff
Walters*	warthog	wat	whop	Zoffany
Walthamstow*	Warwick*	watch	whopped	Zomba
Walton*	was (British RP)	watchband	whopper	zombie
Walton-le Dale*	Wasdale	watchcase	whopping	zonk
waltz*	Wash	watchdog*	whops	Zonta
waltzed*	wash	watcher	wigwam	Zontian
waltzer*	wash-wipe	watches	windowshopping	zonule
waltzes*	washable	Watchet	window-shop	Zoroaster*
waltzing*	washbasin	watchful	window-shopper	Zoroastrian*
Walworth*	washboard	watching	windowshops	zoster
wampum	Washbourn	watchmaker	witnessbox	
wamscot	Washbourne	watchstrap	wobble	
wan	washbowl	watchtower	wobbles	
Wanamaker	Washbrook	watchword	woebegone	
wand	Washburn	Watendlath	wog	
wand	washclo*th	water*	woggle	
Wand	washday	wa*terlog	wok	
wander	washed	Watford		
wandered	washed-out	wath		

BIBLIOGRAPHY

Blunt, Jerry. Stage Dialects. Harper and Row. New York, NY. 1967.

Critchley, Macdonald. The Language of Gesture. MSG House. Brooklyn, NY.

Crystal, David. The Cambridge Encyclopedia of Language. Cambridge University Press. New York, NY.

Lessac, Arthur. The Use and Training of the Human Voice. DBS Publications, Inc. New York, NY.

Linklater, Kristin. Freeing the Natural Voice. Drama Book Specialists. New York, NY. 1976

Linklater. Freeing Shakespeare's Voice. Theatre Communications Group Inc. New York, NY.

The Poems of Gerard Manly Hopkins. eds. W.H. Gardner and N.H. Mackenzie "The Leaden Echo and the Garden Echo" and "The Windhover" by Gerard Manly Hopkins. Oxford University Press. New York, NY.

Morris, William. The American Heritage Dictionary. Houghton Mifflin. Boston, MA

Paget, Richard. Human Speech. AMS Press. New York, NY

Paget. This English. Kegan Paul International Ltd. London, UK.

Rico, Gabriel L. Writing the Natural Way. Jeremy P. Tarcher Inc. New York, NY.

Skinner, Edith. Speak With Distinction. Applause Theatre Book Publishers. New York, NY.

Stern, David Allen. Acting with an Accent. Dialect/Accent Specialists. Los Angeles, CA.

9 780972 745017